The Jossey-Bass Nonprofit & Public Management Series also includes:

THE
Budget-Building
Book *for*
Nonprofits

THE
Budget-Building Book *for* Nonprofits

A Step-by-Step Guide for Managers and Boards

by
Murray Dropkin
and
Bill La Touche

JOSSEY-BASS PUBLISHERS
SAN FRANCISCO

Jossey-Bass books and products are available through most bookstores. To contact Jossey-Bass directly, call (888) 378–2537, fax to (800) 605–2665, or visit our website at www.josseybass.com.

Substantial discounts on bulk quantities of Jossey-Bass books are available to corporations, professional associations, and other organizations. For details and discount information, contact the special sales department at Jossey-Bass.

This book is printed on paper containing a minimum of 10 percent postconsumer waste and manufactured in the United States of America.

Interior design by Paula Schlosser.

Library of Congress Cataloging-in-Publication Data

Dropkin, Murray.
    The budget-building book for nonprofits: a step-by-step guide for nonprofit managers and boards/by Murray Dropkin and Bill La Touche.
        p.   cm.—(The Jossey-Bass nonprofit & public management series)
    ISBN 0-7879-4036-4 (alk. paper)
    1. Nonprofit organizations—Finance.   2. Budget in business.
I. La Touche, Bill.   II. Title.   III. Series: The Jossey-Bass nonprofit and public management series.
HG4027.65.D76   1998
658.15'4—dc21   98-17568
                                                                                        CIP

FIRST EDITION
PB Printing   10 9 8 7 6 5 4

The Jossey-Bass
Nonprofit & Public Management Series

CONTENTS

Dedicated to Thomas H. Gregory, a great friend and mentor

PREFACE

Despite an increasingly complex regulatory atmosphere and shrinking funding sources, the nonprofit sector continues to grow in size and importance. At the end of 1993, there were over 1.1 million tax-exempt organizations in the United States, not including an estimated 527,000 churches. About half of the 1.1 million are 501(c)3 organizations that can receive tax-deductible contributions, with total revenues of $406 billion and total assets of $674 billion. A recent study that excluded religious and political organizations found that nonprofits in the United States employed 7 million people (almost 7 percent of the country's workforce) and made annual expenditures equal to 6.3 percent of the U.S. gross domestic product.

The ways in which nonprofits are supported, regulated, and monitored by government makes them far more complex than comparable commercial organizations in almost every area of operation. Nonprofits are subject to a much wider range and a greater degree of government and private regulation and oversight than are most commercial entities. Thus, nonprofits generally have more complex accounting systems, budgeting processes, auditing procedures, taxation considerations, and financial and organizational management concerns. Moreover, because of financial mismanagement in a small number of organizations, all nonprofits are finding themselves increasingly under the microscope of government and other regulatory agencies. This, coupled with greater competition for funds, has forced many nonprofits to reevaluate everything, from how they conduct day-to-day operations to their overall strategic plans, in order to stay viable. Underlying every aspect of nonprofit operations is the budget. The budgeting process is the foundation on which the nonprofits' long- and short-term health rests. Yet very few resources exist that are written specifically to offer step-by-step guidance to nonprofit managers, boards of directors, financial staff, and the consulting and accounting professionals that serve them, through what can be a very complex process. The purpose of this workbook is exactly that.

Since 1965, we have been assisting small ($100,000), medium ($5 million), and large ($1 billion) nonprofit organizations plan, develop, process, and implement program, capital, operating, departmental, and various other budget programs, analyses, and reports. What we have found, across the board, is that the tools available for budgeting are difficult for anyone other than highly specialized financial professionals to understand; are difficult to apply to the unique circumstances in which many nonprofits operate; or are wonderful in their explanation of the theoretical principles, but do not detail the nuts and bolts of budgeting.

We wrote this workbook to offer nonprofits a comprehensive and systematic approach to developing and monitoring a budget. One of our most important objectives was to create a resource that will be understandable and useful to those with no financial background, as well as those with extensive financial backgrounds. To accomplish this objective, we have incorporated detailed explanations, checklists, worksheets, examples, and simple-to-use forms to address every phase of budgeting. For this reason, we believe *The Budget-Building Book for Nonprofits* will be a practical resource for anyone involved in the budgeting process of small, medium, and larger nonprofits—whether a thorough review of overall budget methodology is needed or just a minor reworking of the discreet problematic aspects of budgets.

The Budget-Building Book for Nonprofits is divided into three practical parts that may be used independently or as a complete sequential package. Part One introduces and provides an orientation to budgeting basics. The chapters in this part present an overview of the common types of nonprofit budgets, the key roles of the various players in developing a budget, overall budgeting strategies, and the effects of different sources of nonprofit revenue on a budget.

Part Two contains information and tools for the hands-on development of budgets and supporting documentation. Some of the elements are step-by-step descriptions and instructions for developing organizationwide and program budgets; developing a budgeting calendar; establishing budgeting goals, priorities, guidelines, policies, and procedures; creating budgeting forms; and estimating and projecting income and expenses. It then details the final steps in the budgeting process, from revising draft budgets to final budget approval. Among the topics are developing and presenting budget proposals to the board of directors, establishing systems for board review and revision of budgets, and monitoring and modifying approved budgets. This part contains checklists, worksheets, and tips for preparing for, navigating through, and streamlining the budgeting process. Our goal is to demystify and systematize budget development.

Part Three contains a diverse collection of sample forms and illustrative materials, including a master form for creating a program or unit work plan, an example of a detailed organizationwide expense budget, and blank samples of budgeting forms for several different types of programs.

In our years of experience dealing with every aspect of nonprofit finances, we have found that nonprofit organizations with effective budgeting practices have a substantial edge in competing for funding over those that do not meet these standards. We believe that the potential exists within every nonprofit to budget effectively and efficiently.

April 1998
New Brunswick, New Jersey

Murray Dropkin
Bill La Touche

ACKNOWLEDGMENTS

We are most appreciative of Allyson Hayden for her extensive editorial, organizational, and creative input.

A number of people gave us their time, effort, and encouragement as we researched, wrote, reviewed, and revised this workbook. We truly appreciate the contributions of David H. Freed, president, Overlook Hospital; Philip M. Henry, publishing consultant and freelance writer and editor; Sylvan Leabman; Kate Miller; Scott Phillips; Edward Kitrosser; Pendar Digges La Touche; Ronald J. Werthman, vice president of finance, treasurer, and chief financial officer, Johns Hopkins Health System Corporation; and Carol Wolff, executive director, Camden Area Health Education Center.

We also are sincerely grateful to Eusebio David, controller, MBD Community Housing Corporation; Theresa Dominianni, partner, Dropkin & Company; C. Roy Epps, president, Civic League of Greater New Brunswick; Eric Havemann and Shirley Dey, Dropkin & Company; Diane Hubka; Wendy Kolb, business manager, Community Legal Aid Society; Kirk Lindsay, controller, Northern Manhattan Improvement Corporation; Ralph Porter, president, MBD Community Housing Corporation; Elizabeth Rosen, controller, Pierpont Morgan Library; Judith A. Schuenemeyer, executive director, Community Legal Aid Society; and Kathryn Talmadge.

We also thank Goldie and Lisa Dropkin, as well as Kit La Touche.

Finally, we are grateful to Alan Shrader and his colleagues at Jossey-Bass for all of their encouragement and help in publishing this book.

THE AUTHORS

Murray Dropkin is the managing partner of Dropkin & Company, Certified Public Accountants, a firm that specializes in working with nonprofit organizations. Dropkin's experience with nonprofit budgeting spans three decades, during which time he has participated in the budgeting processes of virtually every type of nonprofit organization, from child welfare and protection agencies to mental health organizations to theater development organizations to university academic and medical departments. He has trained staff and board members in effective budgeting techniques and has assisted an extensive number of organizations with budget development. Dropkin has published extensively in the field of nonprofit accounting and is coeditor of *Nonprofit Report,* a monthly newsletter. He is the coauthor of the three-volume *Guide to Audits of Nonprofit Organizations,* published annually since 1989. Dropkin earned his B.S. at Brooklyn College and his M.B.A. at New York University. He is a Certified Public Accountant in the states of New York, New Jersey, and Wisconsin and a member of the American Institute of Certified Public Accountants, the Association of Government Accountants, and the New York and New Jersey state CPA societies.

Bill La Touche, a former university teacher and community organizer, is coeditor of *Nonprofit Report.* Over the past thirty years, he has used his writing, planning, training, and organizing skills to help a wide range of individuals, groups, and organizations get what they want from complex business, governmental, and nonprofit entities. He has created numerous training, personnel, self-study, and orientation manuals; employee handbooks; funding and development materials; policy and procedure guides; and public information literature. He has been a fellow of the Institute for Individual and Organizational Development.

INTRODUCTION:
How to Use This Book

*T*he Budget-Building Book for Nonprofits covers the subject of nonprofit budgeting from a practical, hands-on perspective and presents the material so that someone who has never participated in the budgeting process may be able to do so with confidence. We believe as well that even those with extensive budgeting experience or a financial background will find a great deal of helpful information within this book.

Our top priority as we developed *The Budget-Building Book for Nonprofits* was to make it useful and relevant to readers at all levels of financial and budgeting experience. Nevertheless, your own budgeting experience, professional background, and role within the budgeting process will determine how you can best use the book. To help you determine how your organization might use this workbook, we have included descriptions and tips on how readers in different situations might approach and benefit from *The Budget-Building Book for Nonprofits*.

If you are budgeting for a smaller nonprofit, especially one with just one or two programs, this book will be most valuable to senior staff, especially the executive director (or equivalent), the senior financial manager (whether salaried or volunteer), and board members. You can use *The Budget-Building Book for Nonprofits* to establish your entire budgeting process, from beginning to end, or revitalize one you already have. Use it also to educate board members, especially new ones, on the board's role in the budgeting process and how an effective budget is developed. Additionally, this book may be an excellent tool for educating newly hired financial personnel with limited nonprofit experience (those with primarily for-profit backgrounds).

If you are budgeting for a medium-sized nonprofit or one with multiple programs and sources of income, *The Budget-Building Book for Nonprofits* will be useful to senior executives and financial staff for modifying and improving the existing budgeting system. As well, it may be used to orient program and support department managers to budgeting techniques and can be especially helpful for managers new to the organization. As in the case of smaller nonprofits, *The Budget-Building Book for Nonprofits* is a practical tool for orienting financial staff who are new to the nonprofit environment and for new board members.

If you are budgeting for a larger nonprofit, *The Budget-Building Book for Nonprofits* will enrich budgeting processes when it is used to educate program and support department managers about budgeting. As well, this book will be very useful for smaller affiliates and chapters of larger nonprofits that are required to do their own budgeting, but must conform to organizationwide budgeting standards. Furthermore, new financial staff and board members of larger nonprofits will benefit from using *The Budget-Building Book for Nonprofits* to orient themselves to the nonprofit budgeting process.

If you are inexperienced in developing budgets or are unfamiliar with nonprofit budgeting, we recommend that you read *The Budget-Building Book for Nonprofits* in its entirety and in sequential order, starting with Part One, which contains important background information. After reading this part, use the diagnostic budgeting checklist in Chapter Seven to alert you to where you will find the specific information you require to develop your budget. We recommend that you continue to read the book sequentially, paying particular attention to the sections you have highlighted in the diagnostic budgeting checklist. As you read, make notes and jot down the book sections that you find especially helpful. Be sure to review the sample forms, checklists, worksheets, and budget examples found throughout book, especially in Part Three. When you are finished reading the book, use the diagnostic budgeting checklist, the annotated Contents, and your notes to direct you in developing your budget.

If you are experienced in developing nonprofit budgets, we recommend that you at least skim all of the material in *The Budget-Building Book for Nonprofits.* You never know when you might find something to spark a great new idea to use in your budgeting process. Otherwise, start at the diagnostic budgeting checklist in Chapter Seven to navigate to the information that will be most helpful to you. The checklist, as well as several other sections, contain references to information in other chapters that relate to the matter being discussed. You may also use the annotated Contents to find the specific information and tools you need for budget development. *The Budget-Building Book for Nonprofits* is also a good reference to turn to when a particular issue has stalled your budgeting process. Additionally, reviewing the exhibits, especially those in Part Three, might yield an especially useful budgeting or planning tool, which could save you the time of having to create it yourself.

As you go through *The Budget-Building Book for Nonprofits,* you will notice that many sections contain references to other chapters. We have included these cross-references in recognition of the fact that budgeting is not a linear process; rather, it is one in which many aspects and elements are interconnected and interdependent. We think you will find these cross-references very useful in directing you to other relevant information. Additionally, each of the resources in Part Three has its own Contents, listing the exhibits contained in it.

THE
Budget-Building Book *for* Nonprofits

PART ONE

Understanding Budgeting Basics

Why Budgets and Budgeting Are Important to Nonprofits

The dictionary defines "budget" as:

1. "A statement of the financial position of an administration for a definite period of time based on estimates of expenses during the period and proposals for financing them"

2. "A plan for the coordination of resources and expenses"

3. "The amount of money that is available for, required for, or assigned to a particular purpose"

These are pretty long-winded definitions. In plain language, they mean:

- An effective budget is a plan
- For receiving and spending specific amounts of money
- In specific cost categories
- To get specific things done
- Within a set period of time
- With monitoring mechanisms built into the process.

There is an even shorter way of saying this:

A budget is a plan for getting and spending money
to reach specific goals by a certain time.

"A budget is a plan." The word "plan" in this sentence sounds solid and reassuring. In reality, however, most plans are only as good as the work and information that go into preparing them. Basically, a plan is:

- A well-thought-out idea of future actions
- Needed to achieve specific goals
- Within a set period of time
- Based on past experience
- Current information
- And assumptions about the future.

This means that people who prepare budgets and plans must:

Set specific goals . . .

Examine the past, present, and future . . .

And identify the specific actions and costs . . .

Needed to reach the goals they set in the first place.

Four rules about budgets and plans are basic:

Rule 1　A budget is a plan for spending money to reach specific goals by a certain time.

Rule 2　Any budget or plan is only as good as the time, effort, and information people put into it. Good budget practices should foster collaboration and exchange of information among the budget team participants.

Rule 3　No budget or plan is perfect, since none of us can totally predict the future.

Rule 4　In order to reach our goals, all budgets and plans must be monitored and changed as time goes on.

A. The Importance of Budgets and Budgeting

Many nonprofits need budgets to get money in the first place. But even if a funding source is willing to provide funds without a budget, a well-managed nonprofit will still prepare a detailed budget for spending the money. Simply stated, the top priority of any nonprofit should be staying solvent, and budgeting is the optimum tool for promoting this goal. Finally, the more clear, accurate, and well-thought-out budgets are in the beginning, the more likely a nonprofit will be able to:

- Adjust plans, activities, and spending as needed

- Spend money cost-effectively

- Reach the specific goals it has set

- Receive "clean" audits

- Avoid incurring questioned or disallowed costs or cost overruns that it may have to pay for from other funds

Well-prepared budgets have other benefits too. They let everyone in the organization know:

- The goals to be achieved

- The work to be done to reach the goals

- The resources (people and things) needed to get the work done

- The resources available for getting the work done
- The timetable and deadlines for getting specific work done
- The individuals responsible and accountable for doing the required work

Budgets serve additional functions for well-managed nonprofits:

1. Budgets provide the financial and operational guidance needed to implement board policies and directives.

2. Overall, budgets allow management to measure and guide the nonprofit's immediate and long-term financial health and operational effectiveness.

3. Budgets guide a nonprofit's acquisition and use of resources.

4. Budgets anticipate operational expenses and identify income to pay for such expenses.

5. Budgets are tools for controlling spending and avoiding deficits.

6. Budgets help integrate administrative, staff, and operating activities.

7. By monitoring actual income and expenses against those that were budgeted, management can assess the nonprofit's overall financial situation and alter plans as needed.

8. Budgets can serve as the basis for performance reviews and, in some cases, compensation criteria.

B. The Basic Nature of Budgeting

Budgeting is thoughtful and deliberate. It involves carefully setting goals and developing plans, as well as creating a logical and informed process for allocating resources.

Budgeting is inclusive. It brings together the perspectives and interests of a wide variety of groups: the board, clients, management and staff, prospective donors and income sources, and the general public. At the outset of the budget process, input from all relevant parties is sought. Dissemination of the approved budget should clearly and effectively communicate priorities, goals, and operational plans to the entire organization.

Finally, *budgeting is an ongoing process.* It does not occur in a vacuum or for a limited period, producing a document that gathers dust on a shelf. Ongoing monitoring, data gathering, analysis, revised projections and assumptions, and consideration of alternatives are needed.

Over time, careful attention to the budgeting process will lead to greater financial stability, operational effectiveness and efficiency, and responsiveness to organizational needs and priorities.

CHAPTER 2
Understanding Basic Types of Nonprofit Budgets
Overview

Generally nonprofits benefit from using five types of budgets:

1. Total, organizationwide operating budgets
2. Operating budgets for individual programs, units, or activities
3. Capital budgets
4. Cash-flow budgets
5. Opportunity budgets

A. Organizationwide Operating Budgets

Nonprofits with multiple programs or units are most likely to need an organizationwide operating budget. Such budgets identify all the income and expenses anticipated to be needed for the entire organization's operations during the coming year. An organizationwide operating budget should include all the cost for employees, consultants, programs, services, facilities, and other elements needed to organize, carry out, and evaluate the organization's total administration, units, programs, and activities.

To establish and maintain an organizationwide operating budget, nonprofit managers need to spell out the budgeting cycle, budgeting responsibilities, and a detailed schedule or budget calendar. In addition, the board should adopt written budgeting policies to guide the overall process. Usually these policies also describe the economic framework for the budget (for example, setting a standard for the estimated rate of inflation that will be used in computing budget amounts).

The size and complexity of a nonprofit determine to what extent its organizationwide budget will resemble a pyramid, with each succeeding level representing a consolidation of several budgeting units, or cost centers. For example, the lowest level of the pyramid in a large nonprofit's budget may comprise program and activity budgets. The second level will include consolidations of the programs and activities for each unit into unit budgets, which will also include the budget details for the functioning of the unit itself. The third level might consist of the consolidation of all the units in each department or division (and the budget details for the functioning of the department itself) into department or division budgets. Finally, the organizationwide budget tops the pyramid; it contains all department or division budgets and the highest-level organizational budget details.

A small nonprofit without multiple units or departments may present the budget of its one program or activity as its organizationwide budget (assuming it has only one program or activity). However, if it consolidates several unit or activity budgets into an organizationwide budget, each program or activity budget must include a justifiable allocation of overhead and central administrative costs. The reason is that the individual programs serve as cost centers (that is, primary fiscal units) in smaller nonprofits.

For a sample organizationwide expense budget, see Resource E. For more detailed information on creating organizationwide operating budgets, see Chapters Six and Twelve.

B. Operating Budgets for Individual Programs, Units, or Activities

Individual programs or activities within a nonprofit usually require their own specific budgets to gain support from outside donors and other funding sources, as well as to provide necessary budgetary controls. Such individual operating budgets can also help to build the total, organizationwide operating budget.

An operating budget for an individual program, unit, or activity should allow for all the employees, consultants, services, facilities, and other elements needed to organize, carry out, and evaluate operations of a specific program, unit, or activity. Small nonprofits that operate only a single program or have a single purpose, like day care centers, may find they need to create only one program or unit budget, which encompasses the entire organization's operations.

For examples of program or unit operating budgets, see Resource B.

C. Capital Budgets

Capital budgets are tools that nonprofits may use to help plan and manage *capital projects,* those requiring relatively large, one-time expenditures, like buying or constructing a building and acquiring expensive equipment. In many cases, capital projects require funding for more than one fiscal year, which will have to be reflected in capital budgeting. Basically, there are two sorts of capital projects: *capital improvement projects* (used to buy, construct, or extensively renovate physical facilities) and *capital equipment projects* (used to acquire expensive equipment for long-term use). Following are examples of the definitions a nonprofit may use in the capital budgeting process:

1. Capital projects are major, nonrecurring expenditures that are required to support:
   - The purchase, construction, or renovation of physical facilities; or
   - The purchase and/or design of major equipment or systems.

2. Capital improvement projects involve the construction or major renovation of a building or other facility. Typically a capital improvement project has:
   - A useful life of more than one year; and
   - Is over a specified total dollar cost (for example, $5,000, $10,000, or some other amount) that is set by a funding source or the nonprofit.

3. Capital equipment projects involve the purchase of equipment and the services required to make it operational. Capital equipment purchases generally have:
   - A useful life of more than one year; and
   - A specified value (for example, $500, $1,000, or some other amount) established by a funding source or the nonprofit.

The capital budgeting process is primarily concerned with finding the best means of financing capital projects, such as issuing bonds, long-term borrowing, or conducting a fundraising campaign focused on capital needs.

Although this workbook does not deal with developing capital budgets, many of the principles discussed are applicable to the capital budgeting process. For an example of a capital budget, see Resource B.

D. Cash Flow Budgets

Cash flow budgeting is essential to the day-to-day and long-term fiscal health of every nonprofit. Cash flow budgets require organizations to project and describe the schedule, nature, and amount of revenues and expenses. Planning for cash flow management has the same level of importance in a nonprofit organization as overall organization-wide budgeting. Failure to manage cash flow properly can cause severe operational problems.

Stated simply, *cash flow* is the difference in the amount of actual cash coming in to an organization from support and revenue, such as dues, grants, and fundraising, and the amount of actual cash going out of an organization in the form of expenses, such as salaries, rent, office supplies, and other payments. Unfortunately, cash flow analysis is often overlooked by nonprofit organizations until there is not enough cash available to meet outstanding obligations.

Difficulties in cash flow management often result when income lags behind expenditures. For example, some nonprofit organizations are not reimbursed by their funding sources for services rendered until long after the fact. In order to provide these services, expenditures for staff, office space, equipment, supplies, and so forth must often be disbursed before reimbursement is expected to arrive. To deal with this problem, a nonprofit organization must perform proper cash flow planning.

Cash flow budgets project payments (disbursements) and cash received (receipts) month by month over the course of the fiscal year or other period, focusing on the timing of these transactions. A cash flow budget highlights times when gaps are likely to occur, with projected disbursements likely exceeding cash then on hand (a situation referred to as *negative cash flow*). As well, a cash flow budget will show periods when idle cash will be available for investment (referred to as *positive cash flow*). In the case of projected cash shortfalls, a complete cash flow analysis will go one step further by identifying how the shortfall can be avoided so programs can continue without interruption.

Proper cash flow planning requires the preparation of a cash flow projection, which serves as an early-warning device to keep cash reserves from becoming too low to meet cash needs.

For more information on cash flow projection, planning, and troubleshooting, as well as an example of a cash flow budget, see Chapter Eight, Section D, and Chapter Twenty, Section D.

E. Opportunity Budgets

Opportunity budgeting, a term used by Peter F. Drucker in *Managing in Turbulent Times* (HarperCollins, 1980), describes a budgeting process that ideally is used when all of the other types of budgets described in this section are developed effectively. It plans for and examines opportunities for organizations to do something new and different that are most likely to yield the most positive results. For example, organizations interested in opportunity budgeting would prepare an analysis or projection of various possibilities for expansion that would further an organizational mission or improve operations. Then, when it becomes possible to budget for revenue surpluses (or when surplus revenue unexpectedly materializes), the organization would have all of the relevant information and research on hand to make the best decisions about using the revenue as opportunities present themselves. Thus, developing an opportunity budget allows an organization to take advantage of any situation that may result in better fulfillment of an organizational goal or objective.

In order to reap the benefits of an opportunity budget, an organization must have sound budgeting practices; clear, efficient, and realistic planning; and well-conceived strategic goals. These three elements will allow an organization to seek opportunities for expansion—and to budget for them—with the confidence that the structures, resources, and practicality of doing so are in evidence. Of course, there is always an inherent risk in expansion, but when expansion is part of a well-thought-out and timely move, it can reinvent an organization. Actively researching and looking for opportunities that your organization can economically support is one of the most effective growth-promoting tools. Drucker's *Managing for Results* (HarperCollins, 1964) contains many examples of identifying opportunities successfully.

Key Board and Staff Roles and Responsibilities in Nonprofit Budgeting

The roles people play in budgeting generally depend on the nonprofit's size, structure, and income sources. In general, budgets are best developed collaboratively, using the skills and knowledge of those at a number of levels. However, because creating a budget may touch on sensitive or confidential issues, individuals involved in the budgeting process need to know what is expected of them.

The following discussion of some roles that people in various positions within the organization may play in the budgeting process is just one model for budgeting roles; many variations of this model are used successfully by organizations. Whatever division of responsibility is used, the basic requirement is to have and follow a specified process, tailored to the organization and its budgeting goals. Budgeting roles and responsibilities should be spelled out in written policies and procedures, which should be kept up to date and understood by those involved.

A. The Board's Role

The board's role can vary according to its members' willingness and ability to commit time and effort to budgeting. Some boards are deeply involved and participate in planning the annual budget strategy and guidelines, analyzing draft budgets, and giving final approval. Other boards may rely more on management, effectively restricting their role to budget review and approval. Additionally, boards may designate a finance or budget committee with the specific responsibility of working on the budget.

Overall, the board is legally responsible for ensuring that budgets meet applicable laws and regulations, are fiscally sound, and will further the nonprofit's tax-exempt purpose. In larger nonprofits, this generally means:

1. Developing and reviewing the nonprofit's mission statement and its specific goals and activities for achieving the mission.

2. Creating a statement of strategic program and service priorities to guide resource and allocation decisions during the budget process.

3. Establishing general budget policies, such as:
   - Requirements for a balanced budget;
   - Policies on the use of cash reserves; and

- Decisions about salary increases, hiring, layoffs, new programs, capital projects, and major fundraising efforts or capital campaigns.

4. Formally reviewing and approving the budget.

5. Regularly reviewing financial and narrative reports on budget implementation and planning for any needed corrective action. (If possible, this review should include a comparison against external or competitive benchmarks. For example, a child care organization should ascertain what it costs similar organizations to feed a child in day care for one week to determine the accuracy of this budgeted item.)

Of course, an individual board may wish to do more (or less) in the budget development process. Working with and through the chief executive officer (CEO) or executive director, a board could do the following:

1. Help evaluate current programs, assess needs for new programs or services, and develop long-range financial forecasts and operating plans.

2. Establish draft budget guidelines by setting expense and income targets for the nonprofit as a whole or for specific departments or programs.

3. Establish guidelines or formats for the budget document itself.

4. Hold budget information sessions for clients, staff, or contributors.

5. Create a working group to study the budget proposed by staff and recommend modifications to the full board.

B. The Executive Director's or CEO's Role

The executive director (ED) or CEO plays a sustained role in the budget process, usually being responsible for:

1. Arranging and staffing any early strategic planning sessions with the board

2. Preparing options and recommendations to guide budget development

3. Ensuring that the budgeting schedule is met

4. Reviewing draft budgets and making resource allocation decisions

5. Presenting the recommended budget to the board, explaining its provisions and possible consequences, and answering board questions

Depending on the size of the nonprofit and its staff, the ED or CEO may delegate many budgeting tasks to the chief financial officer (CFO) or other managers. However, the CEO always is responsible for ensuring that the budget is accurate, adheres to board policies, and is submitted on time for board review and approval.

Once the budget has been approved, the CEO or ED is responsible for working with the CFO to implement it, which involves:

1. Communicating the approved budget to management and line staff so they clearly understand it

2. Regular financial monitoring to compare actual income and expenses to those budgeted

3. Reviewing financial reports to correct negative deviations from the budget and determining what caused the variance

Finally, the CEO is responsible for communicating the results of financial monitoring and corrective action to the board and seeking its input and approval for needed fiscal or program changes.

C. The Chief Financial Officer's Role

The CFO plays a major and sustained role, often having day-to-day responsibility for coordinating budget development, implementation, and monitoring. Typically the CFO:

1. Creates a budget development calendar and ensures that deadlines are met

2. Communicates budgeting policies and procedures to managers and line staff

3. Establishes the format for draft budgets

4. Develops income and expense forecasts based on reviews of external economic and competitive trends, when applicable

5. Collaborates in setting expense and income targets in line with strategic plan for programs or units

6. Evaluates draft budgets from program or unit managers for accuracy, reasonableness, applicable guidelines, and anticipated resources

7. Discusses draft budgets with the CEO and other managers as needed

8. Writes up recommendations for reducing, increasing, or reallocating requested resources

9. Usually prepares the budget document once the CEO's budget decisions are made and may help present it to the board

After the budget is approved, the CFO often is responsible for implementing financial monitoring, including preparing and analyzing budgeted versus actual income and expense reports for management and board use, and overseeing any corrective actions needed.

D. Program, Unit, or Activity Manager's Role

The involvement of program, unit, or activity managers is essential to developing budgets that accurately reflect reality. Program managers are often best equipped to provide information on current program needs and the costs and effects of reducing or expanding their individual operations. They may also be able to supply the most relevant information when developing budgets for new programs or activities.

Ideally, program and unit managers are responsible for developing draft budgets for their areas, which can mean consulting other staff to evaluate current or new programs, operating costs, and staff and equipment needs. When it comes to carrying out budgets, program and unit managers often are best placed to make resource allocation decisions or recommend changes in activities to meet budgeted expense or income targets.

Program or unit managers may also be responsible for assessing the costs of continuing or expanding current programs, as well as creating new programs or making modifications to conform to budget policies. In addition, they may meet with the CFO or CEO to review draft budgets and explore options for change.

After the CFO informs program and unit managers about approved program budgets, they in turn inform staff about any budget or operational changes. They also review regular financial reports prepared by the CFO, monitor income and expenses, and help develop and implement corrective action plans for their specific areas of responsibility.

E. Departmental Manager's Role

Departmental managers (such as the heads of human resources, development and fundraising, information systems, and facilities) have budgeting roles comparable to those of program and unit managers. Because departmental managers are most familiar with the operations they oversee, they are in a good position to develop budgets for their areas of responsibility, often with the support of others in their units.

F. Other Possible Participants

Depending on the nature of the organization and its management style, a number of others may be involved in budgeting—for example:

- Clerical support staff, to prepare various documents and materials throughout the budgeting process and to understand what is expected in terms of tasks, formats, workloads, and schedules

- Consultants and outside specialists, such as independent auditors and accountants, architects, engineers, bond counsel, and specialists in program areas, who need to know their roles and timetables

- Selected clients and volunteers, who often can provide ideas to improve budgets (and whose involvement may be required by certain funding sources)

- Individuals working in an information systems department, who may be called on to do special analyses quickly

Establishing Budget Guidelines, Priorities, and Goals

Establishing guidelines, priorities, and goals are crucial and frequently overlooked budgeting steps in which the board, CEO, and CFO create the overall context for the coming year's budgeting process. They review the nonprofit's mission, current fiscal status, and projected income and expenses for the coming year. Nonprofits with long-range financial plans usually update them at this time, using current information to project fiscal and program trends likely to affect operations.

Based on their review and the specific budget development strategy they have chosen, the board, CEO, and CFO then set organizationwide operating budget goals for income and expenses for the coming year. The goals they set will be used to help guide the development of the coming year's organizationwide operating budget, as well as individual program and unit operating budgets.

A. Setting Guidelines

The board of directors, the CEO, and the CFO often all participate in establishing policies and guidelines for developing the coming year's budget, including matters related to:

1. Specific program objectives and priorities

2. Income and expense targets or limits

3. Policies governing the creation of new programs or positions

4. Guidelines for existing personnel costs, such as wage increases and fringe benefit rates

B. Identifying Priorities

Effectively identifying priorities is contingent on a thorough understanding of the organization's up-to-date and clearly defined mission statement. An accurate mission statement is necessary to guide programs, especially during planning and budgeting activities, because it summarizes the organization's basic purposes and primary reason for existence. A good mission statement can help the organization do several important things, for example:

1. Set clear organizational and program goals.

2. Make sure current and proposed programs and activities are appropriate.

3. Focus resources productively.

4. Help determine the specific activities and expenditures that should be maintained and the ones that should be reduced or eliminated.

Reviewing the mission statement should be the first step in determining organizational and programmatic priorities. The next step might include an examination of the demographics of the service area, the specific realistic needs of clients, and the actual response to existing programs. Assessing existing programs (and any service gap or problem that becomes evident) using these criteria will provide important information for the identification of priorities. For example, if it becomes clear that a certain program seems to meet community needs perfectly yet has an unexpectedly low rate of use and little community support, a budget priority might be to conduct research to determine the cause of this situation.

C. Setting Organizationwide Goals

The board, CEO, and CFO work together to set total organizationwide operating income and expense goals. They determine the following:

1. The total amount of income the organization as a whole expects to take in during the coming year

2. The total amount the organization as a whole expects to spend to carry out all its activities during the coming year

Total operating income and total operating expenses should generally match. If organizationwide expense goals exceed income goals, meaning that anticipated expenses will exceed anticipated income, then the board, CEO, and CFO have the following options:

1. Increase income and/or reduce projected expenses.

2. Be prepared to take corrective action later (such as cutting budgeted costs or generating additional income).

3. Formally decide to use funds from the organization's unrestricted funds to make up the difference.

4. Take the risk of operating at a deficit during the coming year. We do *not* recommend this choice.

If organizationwide income projections exceed expense projections, meaning that estimated income is more than estimated expenses, then the board, CEO, and CFO have the following options:

1. Adjust the total operating income and expense projections so they match.

2. If the difference is a surplus, let it stand as a hedge against unexpected costs during the coming year.

3. Designate the surplus for future use as needed.

D. Setting Individual Program and Unit Goals

The CFO and CEO should work with managers of each individual program and unit to set program and unit income and expense projections for the coming year, based on the organizationwide income and expense projections. In turn, each program or unit manager should use individual program and unit income and expense projections to guide planning for the nature, staffing, and outcome goals of the specific program or unit (and for the line-item detail within the program or unit operating budget). Total anticipated operating income and expenses for each individual program or unit should match. If they do not match, plans for alternative income generation must be developed or expenses must be cut, or both may be necessary. Developing the discipline and knowledge to perform these steps can make a big difference in the future health of the organization.

CHAPTER 5 How Different Sources and Types of Income Can Affect Budgeting

Sources and types of income may affect a nonprofit's budgets and budgeting processes far more than they might a commercial organization.

A. Unrestricted Funds

Unrestricted funds are those whose use is not restricted to specific purposes by the contributor or funding source. These funds may be:

1. Budgeted for uses and time periods largely at the nonprofit's discretion

2. Assigned to any budget category or line item, using any budget category or line-item titles or definition

3. Reassigned, with budget modifications made according to the nonprofit's internal policies and procedures

B. Contract or Grant Agreement Funds

Income accompanied by a contract or grant agreement often means the following:

1. The use of funds may be restricted to specific purposes, which are spelled out or referred to in the contract or grant agreement.

2. People served by the funded program or activity may have to meet specific eligibility requirements.

3. Specific budget category and line-item titles and definitions may have to be used.

4. Budget flexibility or the time period, or both, for expenses may be limited.

5. Specific procedures and funding source approvals may be required to modify the budget.

6. Compliance with the requirements may be subject to audit.

C. Other Restricted Funds

Funds other than those accompanied by a contract or grant agreement may also have their uses restricted by a donor or funding source, either orally or in writing. Such funds may carry with them similar restrictions as those provided under contract or grant agreement. For example, money donated by individuals for specific purposes, such as purchasing a new vehicle or adding a classroom, would fall into this funding category. As well, funds raised by a group of donors for a particular purpose, such as building a new structure, would be considered "other restricted funds."

D. Income from Trade or Business Activities

Income from a trade or business activity carried on by the nonprofit may have the following potential consequences:

1. Income fluctuations may reduce budget accuracy.

2. Budgeted-to-actual income comparisons may have to be made more often.

3. Income shortfalls may require budgets to be updated more frequently.

4. If enough unrelated business income (UBI) is generated, the nonprofit must budget estimated unrelated business income tax (UBIT) payments. (Unrelated business income is subject to the corporate income tax rate. The definition of what constitutes unrelated business income varies based on the mission of the organization. It is a good idea to consult with a tax adviser for assistance with this complex subject.)

E. Asset-Generated Income

Revenue generated from the nonprofit's existing assets (investment or rental income, for example) can have the same possible effects on budgets and budgeting as income from trade or business activities. Nonprofits must devote particular attention to this budgeting area to ensure that there is proper segregation of income and expenses by the source of the funds used to generate it. Specifically, there must be separate accounting designations for income generated from endowment funds (and from any investments made with them) and income generated from other-than-endowment funds.

Many states have laws spelling out in detail the need for specific identification of income streams or monies meeting the endowment criteria of a specific jurisdiction. Officers and board members of an organization can be held accountable for diversion of income earned on endowment funds.

F. Cash and Noncash Contributions, Including Pledges

Income from cash and noncash contributions, including promises to give (commonly referred to as *pledges*), can have the following effects:

1. Income fluctuations may reduce budget accuracy.

2. Budgeted-to-actual income comparisons may have to be made more often.

3. Income shortfalls may require budgets to be updated more frequently.

G. Funds Requiring a Cash or In-Kind Match

A *cash matching share* is exactly what it says: the nonprofit provides a specific dollar amount of funding from an additional source to support the program or activity in question. A *noncash* or *in-kind matching share* means that instead of providing money, the nonprofit provides goods, facilities, services, or equipment from other sources worth a specified amount to the support of the program. A combined cash and in-kind matching share may be used.

Funding sources that require the nonprofit to put up a program matching share can often mean the following:

1. The nature, amount, and sources of the matching share must be included in the budget.

2. The method of determining the value of a noncash matching share must be described.

3. The required matching share must actually be provided.

4. The nonprofit's compliance with the matching requirements can be subject to audit.

In addition, the IRS has its own income and expense definitions with which nonprofits should become familiar early in the budgeting process.

CHAPTER 6 Strategies for Developing Organizationwide Operating Budgets

Effective budget development depends on having clearly defined strategies for the budgeting process. In preparing organizationwide budgets for the coming fiscal year, multiunit nonprofits often must adjust individual units' draft budgets to meet anticipated resources for the organization as a whole.

Nonprofits that clearly define their budget development strategies and communicate them to unit and program heads can build wide support for budget decisions and avoid time-consuming conflicts and adjustments in the future. Unclear or uncontrolled budget development is likely to create problems. This chapter presents four strategies that can help increase the accuracy and efficiency of budget development:

Strategy 1   Setting annual organizational outcome goals from the top down to guide development of draft program and unit budgets

Strategy 2   Setting annual income and expense targets from the top down to guide development of draft unit and program budgets

Strategy 3   Requesting draft budgets from unit and program heads that show priorities for increased, decreased, and unchanged total budget amounts

Strategy 4   Zero-based budgeting

The first two strategies favor top-down approaches to budget development and thus tend to limit program or unit heads' input. The second two strategies emphasize bottom-up approaches and thus tend to provide program and unit managers with more input. Each strategy has strengths and weaknesses, and elements of each can be combined to suit an organization's needs and style. The sections that follow discuss each of these four strategies and provide worksheets to guide their planning and use.

A. Strategy 1: Setting Annual Organization Outcome Goals from the Top Down

This strategy calls for top management to consult with program and unit managers and appropriate staff before any initial draft budgets are developed.

Defining the overall organization's and specific programs' measurable outcome goals in advance provides a framework for managers and board members to make sure

20

that (1) specific draft budgets and plans for the coming year support and further the established outcome goals and (2) that everyone involved has a clear understanding of what needs to be done.

Top management must assess what resources will be available for the next fiscal year based on the most recent income and expense figures and projections, as well as the outcome goals for the coming year. (The outcome goals may apply to the nonprofit as a whole or to individual programs or activities.)

To be effective, the outcome goals must be both specific and measurable. Many nonprofits require quantifiable *performance measures* or *performance indicators* that will demonstrate achievement of specific outcome goals. Following are examples of outcome goals and performance measures:

Sample Outcome Goals

- Increase the number of weatherized owner-occupied housing units from 350 to 475 over a 12-month period.

- Reduce the average per unit monthly heating cost by 5 percent.

Sample Performance Measures

- The actual number of housing units weatherized.

- Actual reductions in monthly heating costs based on a comparison of heating bills for the same month of the year before and after services were provided.

Sample Outcome Goals

- Develop and implement a model employment skills training program by June 1 of the next fiscal year.

- Provide training in the next 12 months to 250 low-income unemployed persons to improve their chances of job placement.

- Place at least 65 percent of the target population in full-time jobs within two months of completing training.

Sample Performance Measures

- Implementation of the program by the specified date.

- Number of clients enrolled in and completing training.

- Number of clients employed two months after training.

With this strategy, the specified outcome goals become the basis for program or unit managers to develop their draft budgets. Outcome goals and performance measures also contribute to the coming year's overall operating plan, providing a clear statement of what the overall organization intends to achieve and how results will be measured.

Use the worksheet in Exhibit 6.1 to plan when and how to carry out this top-down strategy.

**EXHIBIT
6.1**   Worksheet for Setting Annual Top-Down Organizational Outcome
Goals to Guide the Development of Draft Program and Unit Budgets

1. List top management's initial ideas for the coming year's outcome goals.
   (Consult the organization's written mission statement in developing them.)

2. List when and how top management will present their initial outcome-goal ideas to program and unit managers.

3. List when top management will discuss their outcome goals and get input from unit managers.
   (Gain input before deciding on final recommendations to the board, so as to get additional viewpoints, speed buy-in, and help unite everyone behind final decisions.)

4. After discussion with and input from unit heads, list top management's revised recommendations to the board for the coming year's organizational outcome goals.
   (State desired outcome goals clearly and specifically in order of priority.)

5. List the organization's final, board-approved outcome goals for the coming year.
   (State them clearly and specifically in order of priority.)

Follow-through actions required of those managing the budgeting process:

1. Include the year's board-approved goals in the package for developing draft budgets to be distributed to applicable unit heads.

2. Unit heads must make sure their unit's draft budgets include a brief narrative explaining how continuing activities, new initiatives, or proposed changes in their draft budgets will contribute to the nonprofit's overall goals for the coming year.

3. In deciding on the final budget, top management and board members should use the narrative explanations in each draft budget to help assess the potential merits and contributions of each to the nonprofit's goals for the coming year.

B. Strategy 2: Setting Annual Income and Expense Targets from the Top Down

Under this top-down budget development strategy, top management first sets expense and income targets for the coming year for the organization as a whole and for each individual unit. In this way, units know in advance the income that is available (and the income they are expected to generate) during the coming year. Then each unit can develop a draft budget based on the income and expense targets.

Use the checklist in Exhibit 6.2 to plan when and how to carry out this top-down strategy.

C. Strategy 3: Requesting Draft Budgets from Program or Unit Heads That Show Priorities

This strategy calls for each unit head to prepare three draft budgets for the coming year based on a range of percentage variations determined by top management and the board. There are three steps:

Step 1   Top management decides what the percentage of variation should be between the three total draft budgets, for instance, (a) unchanged from this year's total, (b) 3 percent higher, and (c) 3 percent lower. (In any given year, all three draft budgets may reflect differing rates of decreases, or increases, or whatever combination top management and the board call for.)

Step 2   Each unit head prepares the three draft budgets to reflect the unit's priorities and includes a brief summary within each draft budget of the likely impact the specific changes will have on the unit's operations.

Step 3   Top management and the board adjust each unit's draft budget up or down, depending on the most up-to-date understanding of the coming year's income and expenses, and informed by each unit's perspective on change.

The budget team should use the worksheet in Exhibit 6.3 to help plan, introduce, coordinate, and monitor the use of this approach.

EXHIBIT 6.2   Checklist for Setting Annual Top-Down Income and Expense Targets to Guide Development of Draft Program and Unit Budgets

____ 1. Top management forms a working group.

____ 2. The working group creates:

    a. Reasonably reliable projections of unavoidable (that is, a bare-bones estimate) expenses and desirable or hoped-for expense increases for the organization as a whole; and

    b. A projection of income fairly certain to be received and one of income likely to be received, again for the entire organization.

____ 3. The working group summarizes the fiscal position of the nonprofit as a whole for next year, using the group's expense and income projections as a basis.

____ 4. The working group recommends expense and income targets for all programs, units, and activities, based on estimated resources and expenses.

____ 5. Top management reviews the working group's assumptions, calculations, and targets; makes changes as appropriate; and submits them to the board. (Having the board approve income and expense targets can help avoid potential conflict among managers.)

____ 6. Top management clearly communicates board-approved income and expense targets to managers and unit heads in the package of information on developing draft budgets.

| EXHIBIT 6.3 | Worksheet for Program and Unit Heads to Prepare Draft Budgets Showing Priorities for Increased, Decreased, and Unchanged Total Budget Amounts |

List the percentage variation from this year's unit budget total that top management decides each program or unit head must include in the three draft budgets for the coming year:

1. A total of _____ percent more than this year's unit budget

2. A total of _____ percent less than this year's unit budget

3. The same total amount as this year's unit budget

D. Strategy 4: Zero-Based Budgeting

Zero-based budgeting (ZBB) focuses on the thorough reevaluation of each of an organization's programs, units, and activities to determine if it should be continued (and, if so, how) and included in the next budget. The ZBB process requires that management justify the existence of every facet of the organization; essentially, the ZBB has no built-in assumptions or automatically included items. Those using ZBB are starting the budgeting process from zero (as opposed to using prior budgetary figures to build on in creating the next budget). Another way to think of ZBB is that the process demands an answer to the question: "If this product (activity or unit) were not here today, would we start it?" (Peter F. Drucker, *Managing for Results,* HarperCollins, 1964).

Managers must address more specific questions as well when beginning a ZBB process—for example:

1. Should a given program, activity, or position be continued, or would other activities be more important or appropriate?

2. If the program, activity, or position is justified, should it continue operating in the same manner, or should it be modified?

3. If modified, how will it be modified, when, and by whom?

4. How much should the organization spend on the program, activity, or position being studied?

The next step in ZBB is to require every segment of the operating unit to do the following:

1. Identify the major functions or activities it performs.

2. Answer the above four questions as they pertain to the operating unit.

3. Create alternatives or options based on the answers to the questions.

4. Project anticipated revenues and costs related to each option or alternative.

Exploring and answering these questions can lead management to the following options:

1. Abandon the specific unit, program, or activity, perhaps in favor of other options thought to be more effective.

2. Change, strengthen, simplify, redirect, reorganize, outsource, or otherwise change the existing effort.

3. Make no changes.

Possible Problems with ZBB

Zero-based budgeting can help nonprofits, particularly very well-run ones, improve their efficiency, effectiveness, and productivity. However, it is not a panacea, nor is it particularly easy. The following are potential difficulties that may arise while attempting ZBB:

1. ZBB must have dependable, detailed cost information available from the accounting system (which is not always possible).

2. ZBB often feels very threatening to both managers and staff, since it involves evaluating, making comparisons, and deciding on desired changes.

3. ZBB requires fairly detailed planning and cost calculations and can be made even more difficult and time-consuming if it is introduced organizationwide rather than piloted and phased in over time.

Despite these possible problems, ZBB obviously has many benefits, not the least of which is that it encourages managers to look at a broader range of options than they would if using incremental budgeting (Strategies 1 through 3). Nevertheless, because of the potential difficulties, we recommend that organizations experiment with this technique before applying it in a full budgeting process. Using ZBB initially for just one or two programs will allow for a better understanding of its most beneficial application and its strengths and weaknesses.

Use the worksheet in Exhibit 6.4 to plan when and how to carry out this strategy.

EXHIBIT 6.4   **Worksheet for Zero-Based Budgeting**

1. List by whom, when, and how the ZBB approach will be explained to unit heads and others.

2. Identify the specific training that people in finance and other programs and units will get to understand and implement the ZBB approach.

3. List each of the organization's units, programs, and activities that are to be reviewed and analyzed, along with the level of financial and other resources currently committed to and generated by each.

4. List which individuals in each unit, program, or activity will be sent the appropriate parts of the list for review, analysis, and option building.

5. Describe the various options or models that have emerged from each unit's answering the question: "If we were not already doing this, knowing what we now know, would we do it the same way?"

6. List the anticipated income and costs for each model or option (use varying activity levels when appropriate).

7. Describe whether each specific program, function, or activity should be eliminated, modified, or continued relatively unchanged.

PART TWO

Step-by-Step Budgeting Guidelines

CHAPTER 7

Start with the Budget-Building Checklist

Use the following set of questions to direct your search for specific budgeting information as you begin to develop your budget. If this checklist is your starting point in using *The Budget-Building Book for Nonprofits*, you may want to skim Part One for background information on a particular topic of interest. If you have already read Part One, consider the references to information contained in that section to be an opportunity for solidifying your knowledge base. Although *The Budget-Building Book for Nonprofits* covers many more topics than listed below, this checklist can serve as a guide to the information you will need to begin your review.

A. What Sort of Budget Do You Want to Create?
  1. An operating budget for the organization as a whole?
     If YES, see Chapters Twelve, Fourteen, Fifteen, and Sixteen and Resource D.
  2. An operating budget for an individual program or unit?
     If YES, see Chapters Thirteen through Sixteen and Resource B.

B. Do Funding Sources Require Specific Budget Formats, Categories, or Line Items?
     If YES, you will need a copy of all required budget formats, categories, and line items.

C. What Budget Development Strategies Do You Plan to Use?
  1. Setting annual organizational outcome or goals from the top down to guide development of draft program and unit budgets?
     If YES, turn to Chapter Four, Sections B and C, and Chapter Six, Section A.
  2. Setting annual income and expense targets from the top down to guide the development of draft program and unit budgets?
     If YES, turn to Chapter Six, Section B; Chapter Eight, Sections B and C; Chapter Thirteen, Sections B, C, and D; and Chapter Fifteen, Sections A and B.
  3. Having program and unit heads prepare three draft budgets showing their priorities for increased, decreased, and unchanged total budget amounts?
     If YES, turn to Chapter Four, Section B, and Chapter Six, Section C.
  4. Zero-based budgeting?
     If YES, turn to Chapter Six, Section D.

D. Will Budget Development Involve Various Types and Sources of Funds?
     If YES, see Chapter Five.

E. Do You Need to Create or Update Any of the Following Written Budgeting Policies and Procedures?
1. Basic budgeting policies and procedures?
2. Income projection policies and procedures?
3. Expense projection policies and procedures?
4. Cash flow projection policies and procedures?
5. Policies establishing the fiscal year?
6. Policies for budgeting roles, responsibilities, and authority, or modifying in-house or funding-source budgets?
   If YES, see Chapter Eight.

F. Is Each of the Following Aware of His or Her Responsibilities and Involved in the Budgeting Process?
1. The board and specific board committees?
   If NO, see Chapter Three, Section A.
2. The chief executive officer or executive director?
   If NO, see Chapter Three, Section B.
3. The chief financial officer or controller?
   If NO, see Chapter Three, Section C.
4. Program, service, or unit managers?
   If NO, see Chapter Three, Section D.
5. Any others (such as consultants, volunteers, or clients)?
   If NO, see Chapter Three, Sections E and F.

G. Is There an Up-to-Date Budgeting Calendar?
   If NO, see Chapter Nine.

H. Do You Want to Establish Annual Budget Priorities, Goals, and Guidelines?
   If YES, see Chapter Four.

I. Do You Want to Create an Annual Budget Preparation Package?
   If YES, see Chapter Eleven and Resource F.

J. Do You Want to Orient Program and Unit Managers to Budgeting Requirements?
   If YES, see Chapter Ten.

K. Do You Want to Revise Draft Budgets or Get Some Ideas on How to Trim Them?
   If YES, see Chapter Seventeen.

L. Do You Need to Allocate Administrative and Overhead Costs Among Programs and Units?
   If YES, see Chapter Sixteen.

M. Do You Need to Present a Proposed Annual Budget to the Board?
   If YES, see Chapter Eighteen.

N. Does the Board Need to Review, Revise, and Approve the Final Budget?
   If YES, see Chapter Nineteen.

O. Do You Want to Monitor and Modify the Approved Operating Budget?
   If YES, see Chapter Twenty.

CHAPTER 8

Designing Your Budgeting Policies and Procedures

Projecting income and expenses is easier and the results are more accurate and understandable if written policies and procedures exist to provide program and unit managers with necessary guidance.

A. Basic Budgeting Policies and Procedures

The organization should set out its basic policies and procedures:

1. Identify the specific steps, responsibilities, and timetables in the budgeting cycle and incorporate them into the budgeting calendar.

2. Identify those responsible for preparing and disseminating the budgeting package to be used in preparing budget estimates.

3. Identify the contents and format of:
   - The overall budgeting package to be used in preparing draft budgets
   - The format to be used in preparing draft budgets.

4. Identify the number of actual draft budgets to be prepared by program and unit managers. (Options include one showing estimated increases in income or expenses, or both, one showing no change, one showing estimated decreases in income or expenses, or both; or any combination of these.)

5. Identify those responsible for preparing draft budgets and approving them.

B. Basic Income Projection Policies and Procedures

The organization should set its basic policies on income:

1. Identify those responsible for estimating and for approving proposed changes in income.

2. Set the percentages of change for existing income for program and unit managers to use in preparing draft budgets. (Options are a percentage increase, no change, a percentage decrease, or any combination of these.) Be sure to communicate in advance with all current and potential funding sources regarding any possible changes in funding or eligibility for specific funds.

3. Identify those responsible for estimating and approving the certainty of receiving anticipated income from individual funding sources.

4. Identify the level of certainty needed to include anticipated funds in projected income and preparing program and unit draft budgets.

For more detailed information on income projection, see Chapter Fourteen and Chapter Fifteen, Section A.

C. Basic Expense Projection Policies and Procedures

Expense policies and procedures must be established:

1. Identify those responsible for estimating and approving proposed changes in expenses.

2. Identify the percentages of change for existing salaries, wages, and fringe benefits to be used in preparing draft budgets. (Options are a percentage increase, no change, a percentage decrease, or some combination of these.)

3. Identify the methods for determining changes to existing expenses in preparing draft budgets. (Options are estimating a percentage increase or decrease, determining actual increases or decreases by checking leases and catalogs and negotiating with suppliers and vendors, or both.)

4. Identify the methods for determining the amount of any new expenses. (Options are actually checking with suppliers and catalogs, simply checking other budgets, or both.)

For more detailed information on expense projection, see Chapter Fourteen, Sections B and C, and Chapter Fifteen, Section B.

D. Basic Cash Flow Projection Policies and Procedures

The organization should set basic policies on cash flow projection:

1. Identify those responsible for projecting cash flow and generating and updating monthly cash flow reports for all programs and the organization as a whole.

2. Identify who is to receive cash flow projections and reports on a regular basis.

3. Identify those responsible for identifying, reporting, and taking corrective action to deal with cash flow problems.

4. Identify the reporting and approval authority and process for implementing corrective action.

E. Policies Establishing the Fiscal Year

A nonprofit may choose when its fiscal year will begin and end based on a number of considerations. For instance, many nonprofits choose a fiscal year that coincides with the program or fiscal year of their major funding sources. This approach can greatly simplify the process of "closing" and preparing the necessary accounting entries and financial reports required by the funding source. If a nonprofit has several significant funding sources, each with different reporting requirements, this concept may not be applicable in choosing a fiscal year.

One other factor affecting the selection of a fiscal year is the type and schedule of services provided. A nonprofit that provides seasonally fluctuating programs and activities (such as a summer camp) may select a fiscal year that closes after its busiest season. This timing will benefit the organization by simplifying the process of accruing income and expenses and will allow for staff workload to be distributed more efficiently.

F. Other Needed Policies and Procedures

Other budgeting policies and procedures are also needed, including those dealing with the following areas:

1. Budgeting roles, responsibilities, and authority

2. Modifying in-house and funding source budgets

G. Checklist for Information to Include in Written Policies

Creating a checklist of the specific content headings to be covered in written policy statements can help provide uniform guidance and formats for preparing written policies. Here are recommended topics for such a checklist:

1. Specific name of the proposed policy

2. Two or three sentences describing the purpose of the policy (what it is intended to accomplish)

3. The scope of the policy (including information denoting circumstances, transactions, decisions, and staff members to whom the policy applies, as well as any time or dollar restrictions, and what constitutes an emergency situation in which authorized persons can override the policy and its required procedures)

4. Persons, positions, or groups responsible for writing the proposed policy

5. All persons and groups who must provide preapproval review and input into the proposed policy, such as the following:

- Outside funding sources that require specific actions or procedures in the given policy area (such as a policy on bids to purchase certain kinds or amounts of equipment)
- The corporate attorney (for policies involving legal questions or requiring a legal opinion)
- The independent auditor, regarding government cost principles, special regulatory rules, and other requirements
- The board (usually its review and input are required before it exercises its final approval authority)
- Employees and organizational units that will be most affected by the policy

6. Those responsible for communicating and interpreting the policy to others

7. Those responsible for ensuring compliance with the policy on the part of specific people and units

8. Those with the authority to override or short-circuit the policy's procedures in an emergency situation

9. The responsible parties, means, and timetables for reviewing and updating the policy and its related procedures, as well as changing actual day-to-day procedures and practices to ensure better compliance with the written policy

H. Final Review and Integration

The last part of creating written policies is to review and compare all of the written policies and make any revisions needed to ensure that they dovetail and support each other, and are cross-referenced as needed. As well, training should be planned and implemented to ensure that those who will need to use the policies fully understand them.

CHAPTER 9 Creating Your Budgeting Calendar

The budgeting calendar shows the entire budget development cycle:

1. The key tasks in the budget development cycle
2. The budgeting timetable, including target dates for completing each task
3. Those responsible for accomplishing each task

The budget development calendar should be reviewed each year and revised, based on the previous year's experience and any anticipated changes.

A. Five Steps for Developing the Budgeting Calendar

Following are explanations of the five steps necessary for creating an effective budget development calendar:

1. *List major budget development tasks.* Major budget cycle tasks may vary depending on the size of the nonprofit and the overall budget development strategy it adopts. For instance, larger nonprofits may need lengthy data-gathering and planning processes that include multiple phases and tasks, such as the following:

- Developing guidelines for salary and price increases
- Preparing or updating income and expense estimates
- Reviewing and updating long-range financial and strategic plans
- Establishing income and expense goals for programs and departments
- Developing budget priorities, guidelines, and instructions for the coming year

Smaller nonprofits may require somewhat shorter planning processes and fewer phases and tasks. No matter what the nonprofit's size, however, the CFO's first step is to think through the entire budget development cycle and clearly define what must be done.

2. *Establish overall time frames and specific deadlines.* Deciding when to begin and end the overall budget development process depends heavily on the size of the nonprofit and the complexity of the specific budget development strategy chosen.

Budgeting processes in which program or unit managers actively participate should begin at least seven months before the budget must go into effect. Longer lead times give top management more time to prepare budgeting guidelines, materials, and instructions, and allow unit or program managers more time to develop their draft budgets.

At the same time, however, long lead times also mean that fewer months or quarters of the current year's financial information are available to help project income and expenses into the coming year. Thus, the need for accurate projections based on current financial data must be weighed against the need for a realistic time allotment for completing important budgeting steps.

3. *Identify those responsible for each task.* Establish accountability for completing each budgeting task by identifying the individual responsible for ensuring completion of each required task by the deadline. In this way, everyone knows who is supposed to do what in developing the budget.

4. *Seek review and comment from board and staff.* Board and staff review of and comments on the draft budget cycle and calendar provide two benefits. First, members of the board and staff may identify aspects of the draft budget cycle and calendar that others have overlooked in compiling these documents. Second, they may be able to recognize when deadlines are unrealistic from their individual or departmental perspective. Review by support and clerical staff can also be helpful, because they may be able to provide an accurate estimate of the time required to prepare and duplicate budget development instructions and materials.

5. *Revise and distribute the final budgeting calendar.* In revising and distributing the final budget calendar to the board and staff, it is critical that everyone involved in or affected by the budgeting process be clearly informed of the steps in the process, the budgeting schedule, and what is expected of them. Whenever the budgeting calendar is modified, the changes should be communicated in writing to the same people who received the first draft calendar.

Exhibit 9.1 contains a sample budgeting calendar for a large nonprofit using a calendar year as a time frame.

B. Instructions for Creating an Annual Budgeting Calendar (Using Exhibit 9.2)

1. In chronological order, list each major task in the annual budget development cycle.

2. Add the overall budget development cycle's beginning and ending dates.

3. Add target dates for completing each individual task in the budget development cycle.

4. Add the name of the persons responsible for ensuring that each task is completed.

5. List the deadlines for:
   - Distributing the draft budget calendar to board and staff for their review and written comment
   - Receiving written comments from board and staff
   - Revising and distributing the final budget calendar to board and staff.

EXHIBIT 9.1   **Sample Budgeting Calendar for a Large Nonprofit**

DEADLINE DATE	MAJOR TASKS	RESPONSIBLE PERSON(S)
6/1	Meet to review strategic plans, goals, and objectives.	Board, CEO, and CFO
6/15	Prepare income and expense forecasts and set budget targets, budgeting policies, and procedures; prepare budgeting materials, guidelines, and instructions.	CEO and CFO
7/1	Plan and hold kickoff meeting; present major budget development policies and guidelines, materials, and instructions to unit and program managers.	CFO
8/1	Follow up by giving unit and program managers any needed budget development training and additional materials needed, and by identifying specific Finance Department staff to contact for help.	CFO and finance staff
9/1	Unit and program managers prepare draft budgets and backup documentation by deadline, following policies and instructions.	Unit and program managers
10/1	Consolidate all draft budgets and income and expense projections into one; submit to top management by deadline.	CFO
10/15	Top management reviews draft budgets and discusses them with unit and program managers to arrive at any revisions.	CEO and CFO
11/1	Prepare final, revised overall and unit and program budget documents for presentation to the board.	CFO
11/15	Present budget to board for its review, discussion, modification, and approval.	CEO and CFO
11/30	Incorporate all board-approved changes into final budget documents.	CFO and finance staff
12/15	Distribute approved budget to top management, unit, and program heads, and any other appropriate people.	CFO

EXHIBIT 9.2   **Worksheet for Creating an Annual Budgeting Calendar**

DEADLINE DATE	MAJOR TASK	RESPONSIBLE PERSON(S)

CHAPTER 10

Orienting Program and Department Managers to Budgeting

For an annual budgeting cycle to be efficient and successful, everyone involved must clearly understand the annual budgeting goals, guidelines, procedures, and timetable, as well as specific roles and responsibilities within the budgeting process. Each year, program and unit managers should be oriented to current budgeting requirements through the following three steps:

Step 1 Plan and hold a budgeting kickoff meeting at which the CFO, appropriate finance staff, and program and unit managers review and discuss the budgeting package (budget development goals, calendar, guidelines, forms, worksheets, and instructions). Tips for holding an effective budget team meeting are detailed in Sections A and B.

Step 2 Provide program and unit managers with budget development training and any additional materials as needed.

Step 3 Identify specific finance staff members whom program and unit managers can call on for coaching and help as needed.

A. Budget Team Meeting

To ensure that the budget team meeting accomplishes its intended purpose of orienting staff to budgeting requirements, it is important to plan the meeting carefully. Devoting time and thought to planning will go a long way in fostering productivity during the meeting. The first step upper management should take, and fairly soon after the meeting is announced, is to clarify to all participants the purpose of the team meeting. Additional guidelines for those planning the budget team meeting follow:

1. Team meetings should be for:
   - Making brief announcements
   - Identifying issues and problems
   - Generating ideas and suggestions
   - Holding brief discussions
   - Making decisions
   - Reporting progress
   - Assigning follow-up activities.

2. Team meetings are not the best place for:
- Having long and involved discussions
- Gathering detailed information
- Analyzing problems in detail
- Doing the background work needed to solve problems.

Ideally, most—if not all—fact-finding, analytic, and detailed work should be done by individuals or by small subgroups between meetings. In this way, only the results (and not the time-consuming process) are presented to the entire team during the team meeting. This strategy will free up time for the tasks for which the entire team needs to be present.

B. Practical Considerations for Planning Budget Team Meetings

1. *Plan the meeting space and arrangements.* The configuration of the physical space in which a meeting is held influences the manner in which participants communicate, which ultimately affects productivity. For an egalitarian meeting and one that encourages participation of all members, consider a round table or several tables set up in a U or a square. This will ensure that members have equal access to one another and any displays. Avoid any seating arrangement that might be described as a classroom setting.

2. *Set the length of the overall meeting.* With few exceptions, meetings should not last more than one to one and a half hours. This time frame is the upper limit of most adults' productive attention span. Let the budget team know in advance how long the meeting will be, and stick to the time limit. This conveys respect for everyone's time and encourages participants to be concise and direct.

3. *Prepare a written agenda with time limits for each item.* A written agenda is an essential tool for maintaining focus and efficiency during a team meeting. It should be as specific as possible, with realistic time allotments assigned for each task on the agenda. When assigning time limits, keep in mind that giving information takes the least time; generating ideas takes longer; discussing an issue takes even more time; and group decision making usually takes the most time of any task.

CHAPTER 11
Contents of the Annual Budget Preparation Package

Preparation of an annual budgeting package for distribution to those with major budgeting responsibility is usually overseen by the CFO or other top-level financial manager. At a minimum, each budget preparation package should include the following elements:

1. Completed program and unit budgeting instructions and guidelines forms. (See Exhibits 11.1 and 11.2 for worksheets and sample forms.)

2. An updated budgeting calendar. (See Chapter Nine for information on creating or updating the budgeting calendar.)

3. A copy of a blank program or unit work plan. (See Resource A for a sample blank work plan.)

4. Appropriate blank budget forms. (See Resource B for a variety of blank budget forms.)

5. A copy of a blank form for summarizing proposed budget changes. (See Chapters Seventeen and Twenty, which address budget modifications.)

6. Budget assumptions and highlights. (See Chapter Fifteen, Section D.)

7. A letter of transmittal. (See Chapter Eighteen, Section A.)

8. A reference copy of this workbook.

Furthermore, the CEO or CFO should consider providing a short written overview describing budgeting perspectives, unique circumstances, directives, instructions, and any other information that might be useful to those participating in budgeting. For an example of such a letter, see Resource F. In addition to the resources listed above and the exhibits in this chapter, Resource B contains the following samples of blank budget formats to aid in the development of budgeting forms:

1. A blank organizationwide budget format for a community services organization

2. Blank program and unit budget formats for:
   - A museum curatorial department
   - A building and security department
   - A membership department

| EXHIBIT 11.1 | Program or Unit Budgeting Instructions and Worksheet |

I. YOUR ANNUAL PROGRAM OR UNIT GOALS

A. List your specific program and unit outcome goals:

(See page 52, Section C, for more information on developing outcome goals.)

1. _____
2. _____
3. _____
4. _____
5. _____

(Attach additional sheets as needed.)

B. List your related program and unit activity goals:

(See page 52, Section C, for more information on developing activity goals.)

1. _____
2. _____
3. _____
4. _____
5. _____

(Attach additional sheets as needed.)

II. PROGRAM OR UNIT BUDGET GOALS

A. Total income goal: $ _____

B. Total expense goal: $ _____

- A budget form with instructions
- A museum exhibition

3. Blank examples of formats for:

- A capital project budget
- A capital budget for a building

**EXHIBIT
11.2**   **Budgeting Guidelines for Programs or Units**

A. **Draft Budget to Be Prepared (Check one that applies.)**

☐ Prepare ONE draft program or unit operating budget based on the budget goals.

☐ Prepare TWO draft program or unit operating budgets: one based on the budget goals and one on a total amount that is _____ percent lower/higher. (Circle one.)

☐ Prepare THREE draft program or unit operating budgets: one based on the budget goals, one on a total amount that is _____ percent higher than the budget goals, and one on a total amount that is _____ percent lower.

B. **Salary and Wage Increases to Be Applied**

☐ Adjust the wages and fringe benefits of existing employees to reflect a _____ percent increase as of each employee's anniversary date.

C. **Changes in Fees**

☐ The board has authorized an increase of up to _____ percent for programs or units that need to increase income by adjusting fees charged for goods or services.

☐ Please check here if your program or unit is proposing to increase any fees charged for goods or services as a way to increase income for the coming year.

☐ If your draft budget includes any increase in fees for goods or services, please specify the following in your transmittal page:

1. Kind and amount of each fee to be charged.

    a. _____ : $ _____
    b. _____ : $ _____
    c. _____ : $ _____
    d. _____ : $ _____

2. Amount and percentage of increase for each fee:

    a. _____ : + $ _____ (____ percent)
    b. _____ : + $ _____ (____ percent)
    c. _____ : + $ _____ (____ percent)
    d. _____ : + $ _____ (____ percent)

3. Total amount of each fee you expect to bill:

    a. _____ : $ _____
    b. _____ : $ _____
    c. _____ : $ _____
    d. _____ : $ _____

4. Total amount of each fee you expect to collect:

    a. _____ : $ _____
    b. _____ : $ _____
    c. _____ : $ _____
    d. _____ : $ _____

EXHIBIT 11.2   Budgeting Guidelines for Programs or Units _(continued)_

5. Expected fee totals compared to last year:

Fee	Next Year	Last Year
a. _____	$_____	$_____
b. _____	$_____	$_____
c. _____	$_____	$_____
d. _____	$_____	$_____

D. New Programs, Positions, and Employees

☐ _Any new programs_ must be discussed with and approved by the CEO and CFO prior to presenting draft budgets.

☐ _Any plans to fill existing positions that currently are empty_ must be discussed with and approved by the CEO and CFO prior to taking any action.

☐ _Any plans to create any new positions_ must be discussed with and approved by the CEO and CFO prior to taking any action.

CHAPTER 12 Developing Organizationwide Operating Budgets

There are ten steps to creating, implementing, and managing an annual organizationwide operating budget comprised of individual program or unit operating budgets. The first five steps pertain to preparation for the annual budgeting process; the second five concern the actual creation of the annual organizationwide operating budget. Following are brief descriptions of each step, with the persons usually involved in performing the step noted in parentheses. The chapters that contain a more detailed look at the specific aspect of budgeting are identified following each step.

Those involved in the budgeting process may decide to use all or some of these steps, selecting and modifying the tasks and activities in each to suit their organization's unique circumstances.

A. Five Steps to Prepare for the Annual Budgeting Process

Step 1   Selecting a Budgeting Strategy (Board, CEO, CFO). The CEO, CFO, and board should choose a budget development strategy that they deem best suited to their organizational structure, the budget development timetable, the strategic plan, and their management style. Chapter Six describes four basic budget development strategies.

Step 2   Developing Next Year's Budget Goals and Guidelines (Board, CEO, CFO). This is a crucial and frequently overlooked step in which the board, CEO, and CFO create the overall context within which budgeting for the coming year will take place. They review the nonprofit's mission, its current fiscal status, and its projected income and expenses for the coming year. They then establish any budget guidelines and outcome or goals needed to help guide the development of the coming year's budget. For more on this step, see Chapter Four.

Step 3   Creating the Annual Budgeting Calendar (CFO). This next step, developing a detailed budgeting calendar, is described in Chapter Nine.

Step 4   Creating Budgeting Forms, Materials, and Instructions (CFO). To develop their annual operating draft budgets, program and unit managers need a budgeting package that includes blank forms, instructions, and guidance regarding income and expense targets and constraints for the coming year. The CFO is responsible for ensuring that the needed budgeting package is developed in line with the budgeting calendar deadline. For more information, see Chapter Eleven.

Step 5   Orienting Managers to Budgeting Goals and Process (CFO, Finance Staff). The CFO and finance staff must communicate and discuss annual budget development forms, guidelines, and timetables with program and unit managers, who need to understand fully the budgeting package and what is expected of them. It may be helpful to have a budget kickoff meeting that includes all managers responsible for developing draft budgets, the CFO, and key finance staff. For more information, see Chapter Ten.

B. Five Steps to Create Annual Budgets

Step 6   Preparing Draft Program and Unit Budgets (Managers). Each unit or program manager uses the budget development package to develop and submit a line-item draft budget for the next year, based on specific program or unit budgeting or outcome goals. For more information, see Chapters Four and Thirteen.

Step 7   Reviewing and Revising Draft Program or Draft Unit Budgets (CFO). When all draft budgets are received, finance staff should prepare a summary total of all the requests to give management a picture of the resources requested by program and unit heads. Finance staff also should review all draft budgets to ensure that they have been properly and accurately prepared, and to identify issues and changes likely to have a significant fiscal or programmatic effect. Based on these reviews, the CFO or other fiscal staff may prepare internal reports on each budget. These reports should identify issues, options for changes, and fiscal staff recommendations. From this summary, the CEO and CFO can determine if draft budgets must be trimmed and, if so, by how much. After draft budgets have been revised, the CFO should meet with each program or unit manager to discuss individual draft budgets and top management's revisions. For more information, see Chapter Seventeen.

Step 8   Preparing and Submitting a Proposed Budget to the Board (CFO, CEO). Based on results of the draft budget review, the CFO prepares a proposed organizationwide operating budget for submission to the CEO and then the board. After the CEO approves the proposed budget, support staff prepare the budget proposal and any necessary supporting documentation, and the CEO or CFO presents it to the board. For more information, see Chapter Eighteen.

Step 9   Reviewing, Revising, and Approving Final Budget (Board). The board reviews the proposed organizationwide budget and evaluates the extent to which it is likely to achieve the outcome goals and income and expense targets set at the beginning of the budgeting process. Board members may need additional information or may wish to explore alternatives to proposed budget provisions with the CEO or CFO. The board should handle budget changes or amendments as specified in the nonprofit's policies or bylaws. The CEO and CFO should clearly identify the potential effects of any board revisions before the board approves the final budget for the coming year. For more information, see Chapter Nineteen.

Step 10   Implementing, Monitoring, and Modifying Budgets (CFO, Finance Staff, Managers). The final approved budget is distributed to relevant program and unit managers and finance staff. It may be necessary to orient program and unit managers to the approved budget to ensure they understand it and can plan for any needed changes to program and support operations. Finance staff then incorporate the approved budget into the nonprofit's accounting and financial reporting systems. The CEO and CFO at their levels, and the unit and program managers at theirs, are responsible for implementing the approved budget and carrying out all required financial reporting, monitoring, and corrective action, which can include modifying budgets. For more information, see Chapter Twenty.

Developing Operating Budgets for Individual Programs, Units, or Activities

P rogram or unit managers are often responsible for preparing annual draft budgets for their individual programs or units, with assistance from finance staff, review and revision by the CFO and CEO, and final approval by the board. Because of their training and experience, a nonprofit's auditors may also be useful in providing technical assistance in preparation of detailed program or unit budgets.

Each nonprofit should have a step-by-step written approach for program or unit budgeting, so everyone involved knows who does what and when. Program and unit managers may use the worksheet in Exhibit 13.1 to aid in planning for program and unit budget development.

A. Planning for Program or Unit Budget Development

A top manager, the program or unit head, and a finance staff member work together in preparing budgets. To succeed, they should develop a plan and clarify responsibilities at the outset. Here are seven suggested steps for doing this:

Step 1 Agree on Program or Unit Basics. A manager (executive director, assistant director, or director of programs) meets with a program or unit head (program director, services coordinator, or program developer) and a finance person (CFO, controller, or business manager) to discuss and agree on the basics of the proposed program or program renewal.

Step 2 Clarify the Program or Unit Head's Responsibilities. The manager assigns the program or unit head the responsibility for developing next year's program goals, a detailed program work plan, and an outline of basic budget items and estimated costs.

Step 3 Clarify the Finance Person's Responsibilities. The manager assigns the finance person the responsibility for reviewing the contents of the final, detailed budget.

Step 4 Create Draft Program or Unit Goals and Work Plan. The program or unit head develops a draft of program or unit goals and a draft work plan for the coming year.

| EXHIBIT 13.1 | Planning Worksheet for Preparing a Program or Unit Budget |

BACKGROUND

    1. Organization: _____

    2. Program or unit to be budgeted for: _____

    3. Specific program or unit goals to be budgeted for: _____

        a. Outcome goals: _____

            _____

            _____

        b. Activity goals: _____

            _____

            _____

BUDGET PREPARERS

    4. Person(s) primarily responsible for preparing budget:

        a. _____

        b. _____

        c. _____

DEADLINES

    5. Budget due for board review on: _____

    6. Board review, revision, and approval: From _____ to _____

    7. Budget developers should first meet on: _____

    8. Each budget preparer's responsibilities:

        a. _____ : _____

        b. _____ : _____

        c. _____ : _____

Step 5   Review and Revise Program or Unit Goals and Work Plan. The manager and program or unit head review and discuss the draft program or unit goals and work plan, revising them as needed.

Step 6   Identify Budget Categories, Line Items, and Costs. The program or unit head meets with the finance person to identify basic budget categories and line items, as well as estimated costs. The finance person, in conjunction with the manager, then prepares a detailed program budget from this basic outline, using the budget format and guidelines of any relevant funding sources as required.

Step 7   Agree on Final Program or Unit Budget. The manager, finance person, and program or unit head meet to review, discuss, and revise the final program or unit budget, which is then submitted to the CEO and CFO.

B. Basic Steps in Creating a Program or Unit Budget

The following six basic steps may be used to create a detailed program or activity budget:

Step 1   Identify Anticipated Sources and Amounts of Income.

Step 2   Set Specific Goals for the Program or Unit.

Step 3   Prepare a Detailed Work Plan for Reaching the Goals.

Step 4   Identify All the Resources (Employees, Consultants, Facilities, and Supplies) Needed to Implement the Work Plan.

Step 5   Determine the Costs of All Resources.

Step 6   Prepare the Budget.

C. Setting Two Kinds of Program or Unit Goals

In program or unit planning and budgeting, there are two basic kinds of goals: outcome goals and activity goals.

Outcome goals are measurable statements of what a program or unit is expected to accomplish during the coming year (that is, the specific results it should achieve). Following is an example of an outcome goal:

> To enable 50 potential high school dropouts entering tenth grade to complete high school within three years.

This is an outcome goal because it states the specific, measurable results desired for specific people by a certain time.

Activity goals are measurable statements of activities or services that will help the program reach its outcome goals. They do not identify results; they only identify activities that can lead to results. Following is an example of an activity goal:

> To provide an average of 350 hours of after-school tutoring and counseling to each of 100 potential high school dropouts during each year of the project.

This is an activity goal because it is a specific, measurable statement of activities (tutoring and counseling services) that will be carried out within a set time to help reach the desired outcome or goal.

D. Preparing a Program or Unit Work Plan

Once program goals are stated as outcome goals, activity goals, or both, the next step is to identify what must be done to reach them. This means identifying all the action steps needed to organize, carry out, and evaluate the specific program or unit, as well as identifying the target date and those responsible for each action step. Exhibit 13.2 shows a partial example of a work plan that might be created for a program with the outcome and activity goals listed in Section C above.

EXHIBIT 13.2   Sample Program or Unit Work Plan

Action Steps	Responsible Person	Target Date
1. Recruit, screen, hire staff.	Project director	Week 4
2. Orient and train staff.	Project director	Week 5
3. Establish written eligibility criteria.	Project staff	Week 6
4. Design intake forms and procedures.	Counselors	Week 6
5. Make initial contacts with schools for referrals.	Recruiter	Week 6
6. Reach agreement with four schools for referrals.	Recruiter	Week 8
7. Orient school staff to eligibility criteria and referral procedures.	Recruiter	Week 10
8. Design outreach and recruitment activities and materials.	Recruiter and project director	Week 9
9. Begin ongoing outreach and recruitment.	Recruiter	Week 10
10. Begin accepting referrals and walk-ins.	Counselors	Week 10
11. Screen referrals and walk-ins for eligibility (ongoing).	Counselors	Week 12
12. Enroll minimum 15 eligible students per month (ongoing).	Counselors and recruiter	Months 4–11
13. Help enrollee create individual plan by 4 weeks after enrollment (ongoing).	Counselors	Months 4–12
14. Help enrollee begin implementing plan by sixth week after enrollment (ongoing).	Counselors	Months 5–13
[These are only some of the action steps for a program or unit work plan. A complete work plan would include action steps for all program or unit activities, up to the final action step below.]		
37. Prepare and submit final program evaluation and financial reports.	Project director/ CFO	Month 36

To create a program or unit work plan using the Blank Master for Creating a Program or Unit Work Plan, turn to Resource A and review the instructions.

Following are some of the benefits nonprofits can gain from preparing detailed program or unit work plans:

1. Increased accuracy of the program or unit budget

2. Greater opportunities for managers to think through and clearly describe the action steps they will follow to achieve their program or unit goals

3. Greater ability to convince funding sources that the nonprofit is worth supporting

4. Increased understanding of and focus on what needs to be done, when, and by whom for newly hired managers and staff

5. Greater ease for management and staff monitoring of progress through the designation of target dates, which will facilitate program and fiscal adjustments in response to the problems that inevitably arise

E. Identifying People and Things Needed to Implement a Work Plan

Program or unit budgets should allow for all the people, things, activities, and costs needed to organize, carry out, and evaluate a specific program or unit. Once the program work plan has been completed, review it and begin listing the specific positions and things needed and what each will cost. If the budget in development will include a new program or make significant changes to an old program, see Resource F for a sample Program Change Request Form.

Program or unit budgets usually show planned expenses organized by general cost categories ("Consumable Office Supplies," for example), with specific line-item costs (such as those for "Photocopy paper") listed under each category. Sometimes funding sources identify the specific cost categories and line items they expect funding recipients to use in preparing a budget. At other times, they may just give general guidance, leaving it up to the nonprofit to decide the specific categories and line items.

Examples of various kinds of program or unit budget outlines are provided in Resource B. Generic outlines like these should be used only when a potential funding source does not provide its own set of cost categories and line items. If the program or unit budget outlines are used, they should also be carefully tailored to allow for the specifics of the particular program or unit being budgeted.

F. Identifying Personnel Costs

First, list the numbers and titles of personnel needed to carry out the program or unit work plan:

1. Administrative and fiscal and bookkeeping staff.

2. Supervisory staff.

3. Direct service staff.

4. Clerical staff.

5. Other staff (if applicable).

6. Consultants and professional (or contract) services. This group should be listed by specific functions or areas of expertise, such as medical, education, psychiatric/psychological, legal, accounting, employment, data processing or management services.

If a change in staffing will be included in the coming year's budget, check Resource F for a sample New Position Request Form.

Second, write down the salaries and percentages of time each of the above staff members will be employed in the program, with 100 percent being full time. For consultant and professional or contract services, include the numbers of hours or days of service needed, the hourly or daily rate for each function or area of expertise, and the total amount involved for each.

Next, list employee fringe benefits, including those required by law, such as Federal Insurance Contributions Act (FICA) tax, State Unemployment Insurance (SUI), and workers' compensation, as well as any other fringe benefits provided, such as medical insurance. (Be sure to differentiate between fringe benefits that part-time employees get and fringe benefits that only full-time employees receive.)

G. Identifying "Other Than Personnel" Cost Categories

The rest of the budget usually consists of "Other Than Personnel Costs," and includes broad cost categories for equipment, supplies, facilities, and other items needed to carry out the program. Such cost categories may include some or all of the following:

1. Consumable materials and supplies, including office, medical, training, vocational, recreational, laundry, housekeeping, food and beverages, and other program supplies

2. Facilities, including offices and other facilities for implementing the program, and their annual rental, maintenance, and renovation costs

3. Insurance, including insurance for facilities, vehicle, and travel-related insurance and any other kinds of program or activity insurance (but not insurance provided to employees as fringe benefits)

4. Specific assistance for clients, which could include allowances or other cash payments and personal items (such as health and beauty aids for maintaining hygiene, clothing, and personal appearance)

5. Travel and transportation, including client transportation, staff travel, and costs involved in acquiring and operating any vehicles

6. Rental, lease, or purchase of equipment, including office equipment, computer hardware and software, and other program equipment

7. Printing and reproduction, including photocopying and printing

8. Communications, including telephone and postage costs

9. Training, conferences, and meetings, including training for staff or clients and meetings and conferences for disseminating technical information about the program

10. Membership dues for trade, business, professional, or technical organizations

11. Subscriptions to professional journals or other publications needed for the program

12. Miscellaneous goods or services not identified earlier

Some funding sources require recipient programs to use particular methodology and nomenclature when assigning expense categories. For example, one funding source may require insurance costs to be listed under the general category of "other costs," while some may require insurance costs to be listed in its own specific category. Check specific funding source requirements when developing budgets to make sure each budget conforms.

H. Identifying Specific Line-Item Costs

In identifying costs for specific line items under each budget category, use past experience and recent budgets for other programs to help identify similar costs. Catalogs list prices for items and services, and vendors can be asked to supply cost quotations for specific goods and services. For example, contact the telephone company for installation and basic monthly charges, insurance agents for the cost of needed coverage, consultants for the cost of their services, and food wholesalers to get the prices in advance for large food and beverage purchases.

I. Providing Budget Justification or Cost Documentation

Funding sources and budget reviewers often require explanations of line-item costs, which may be referred to as "budget justification," "budget detail," or "documenting costs." Exhibit 13.3 shows some examples under the budget category of travel.

EXHIBIT 13.3   **Justification of Travel Expenses**

STAFF MILEAGE: $1,950

(Estimated 10 round trips per month × 12 months between Springfield headquarters and Lambertville satellite by private auto at 50 miles each trip × 32.5 cents per mile.)

CLIENT TRAVEL: $12,000

(Rent 50-seat bus for 1 round trip a week between Lambertville and Springfield to attend job training classes for estimated 48 weeks at $250 per trip.)

CONFERENCES AND CONVENTIONS: $2,000

(Four round-trip airfares from Springfield to Denver, Colorado, at $500 each for professional development conference on "Exemplary Programs for Increasing High School Graduation Rates.")

As these examples show, budget justifications or cost documentation are simply explanations of (1) what you are going to spend money on, (2) how you arrived at the total figure for a specific line item, and (3) for what purpose each line item will be used. See Chapter Fourteen, for more on budget justification.

J. Matching and In-Kind Contributions

Budgets are sometimes required to show matching contributions or in-kind contributions. *Matching contributions* are resources the nonprofit may be required to provide in order to qualify for the funds being requested in the budget. Matching contributions may have to be in cash or *in-kind*, that is noncash resources like staff, goods, or services. Matching and in-kind contributions are usually listed as specific line items under appropriate cost categories and are explained like any other part of the budget. They should be clearly identified, so the reader will realize they are not requests for support. (Matching and in-kind contributions must also be listed as revenue in the appropriate part of the budget.) See Chapter Five for more information.

K. Who Needs Copies of Final Program or Unit Budgets?

Copies of final program budgets should be distributed to those who:

1. Are responsible for a program or unit, or for the resources used in a program or unit

2. Make decisions that affect the use of resources (resources include people's time and activities; equipment, facilities, and supplies; and expenses)

3. Keep track of expenses or results

4. Are involved in program or unit planning, decision making, or reporting

Obviously, this includes supervisors, middle managers, and top management, as well as important service providers and fiscal and bookkeeping staff. After all, if "a budget is a plan for spending money to reach specific goals by a certain time," then everyone involved needs to know what the plan is. In our opinion, keeping budget information confidential is impossible and in fact defeats the purpose of good budgeting.

CHAPTER 14
Major Components of Operating Budgets

Detailed operating budgets include anticipated income by source and amount, the amounts of individual line-item expenses, and totals by major budget categories (such as salaries, fringe benefits, supplies and materials, and equipment). Each draft budget should also include a summary of budget highlights, explaining any changes in income, expenses, programs, and services; any actions affecting personnel (such as raises, promotions, and creating or eliminating positions); and any other changes to the current budget or current operations. Ideally, the draft budget includes information to substantiate it (for example, an itemized list of requested equipment with individual prices or discussion of increases in costs), which is often known as *budget detail* or *budget justification*.

A section on budget highlights, with examples, may be found in Chapter Fifteen.

Following are brief discussions of the major components of a draft operating budget.

A. Projected Income

Budgets include projected income by sources and amounts and explain any assumptions used to make each income projection. See Chapter Fifteen for detailed information, worksheets, and examples on projecting income.

B. Projected Expense Categories and Subcategories

Budgets include a summary of requested expenses by various account categories and subcategories, with subtotals given for each category. When creating budgets, use the budget categories and subcategories that are required by your organization or an individual funding source. Chapter Fifteen details expense projection techniques.

C. Projected Expenses by Line Item

Under each account category, the budget should identify specific expense line items and amounts, as in the following example of line items under the budget category "Insurance Costs":

- Directors' and Officers' Insurance (covers board members and officers against liability from their official duties; $300 per month ×12 months): $3,600

- General Liability Insurance (protects nonprofit for liability from facility use and employee work-related actions; $500 per month ×12 months): $6,000

- Comprehensive Insurance (fire, theft, and damage from "acts of God"; $200 per month×12 months): $2,400

- Vehicle Insurance (protects nonprofit and employees when operating motor vehicle as part of their duties; $1,250 per month ×12 months): $15,000

    Subtotal, Insurance: $27,000

D. Budget Narrative or Justification

Where feasible or required, a budget may also include written narrative detail to explain and justify its figures, including how specific income or costs were calculated and explanations of significant increases or decreases. For more information, see Chapter Thirteen, Section I.

Estimating Income and Expenses

Accurately estimating income and expenses six months to a year in advance can be challenging, especially when many variables and unknown factors can affect a nonprofit's income stream and costs. Developing any budget requires the following three steps:

Step 1 Carefully estimating the coming year's income from various sources

Step 2 Carefully estimating the expenses needed to operate for the coming year

Step 3 Preparing a summary of budget highlights, so top management and the board can understand the program or unit's priorities and perspectives

A. Estimating Future Income

Estimating future income is difficult for many reasons. However, projecting income is easier and more accurate if some basic annual policy decisions are made early in the process. Exhibits 15.1 and 15.2 are relevant to the process of estimating income.

1. Annual Policy Decisions Needed

a. Policies Regarding Speculative Income. Decide whether the budget will include income the nonprofit has a chance of receiving but for which it has not yet received a firm commitment. Speculative or uncertain income may include grants for which applications are pending or not yet submitted, promises of future contributions (pledges), income from new and untried programs or services, or the results of future fundraising efforts. In addition, those who are developing budgets should always understand that income that has been approved by a funding source may be subject to reduction before it is actually received.

Such income should be clearly identified as uncertain, the estimated percentage of certainty of receiving it should be determined, and any costs to be met with such uncertain income should be clearly earmarked and controlled.

b. Changes in Service Fees. Another common budgeting policy issue involves deciding if new service fees will be charged or if existing fees will be increased and, if so, what those fees will be. Many nonprofits charge fees (often on a sliding scale) to offset the costs of providing services. (Any nonprofit planning to charge fees for the first time or to increase existing fees should be sure that existing or potential funding sources do not prohibit this.)

Determining fees may require analyzing service unit costs to determine the expense of the relevant services per unit. Similarly, market research may be needed to determine whether clients can and will pay the fees, whether fee changes are likely to reduce the number of clients and therefore the number of services provided, and how the amount of income gained from providing the services will be affected by the fee change.

2. Projecting Various Kinds of Income

Ways to project income vary according to the sources and nature of income. However, no matter what the source and nature, it is important to document the assumptions used to prepare income projections. Often income projections need to be revisited and revised during the budget development process. When there is a thorough record of the original assumptions, double counting possible fee increases or additional grant funds, and other potential mistakes may be avoided. Documenting assumptions also can help explain the budget to the board and others.

1. For grant or contract income, reliable income projection indicators might include:
   - The actual income and estimates previously provided by funding sources
   - Funding source payment schedules
   - The status of current negotiations for continued or new contracts or grants.

2. For ongoing or special fundraising campaigns, possible income indicators can include:
   - Prior years' experience
   - Current pledge collection rates
   - Net income after expenses from any other fundraising activities.

3. For income from fees and charges, income indicators include:
   - Prior years' actual experience
   - Any adjustments to fee amounts
   - Expected service levels or caseloads.

B. Estimating Expenses

As with income projections, estimating expenses also requires policy decisions early in the process and specific ways of handling each type of expense projection.

EXHIBIT 15.1	Worksheet for Identifying Sources, Types, and Amounts of Funds

---

1. From fee-for-service contracts:

SOURCE	AMOUNT	LIKELIHOOD OF FUNDING
a. _____	$_____	_____ percent
b. _____	$_____	_____ percent
c. _____	$_____	_____ percent
d. _____	$_____	_____ percent
Subtotals:	$_____	_____ percent

2. From grants:

SOURCE	AMOUNT	LIKELIHOOD OF FUNDING
a. _____	$_____	_____ percent
b. _____	$_____	_____ percent
c. _____	$_____	_____ percent
d. _____	$_____	_____ percent
Subtotals:	$_____	_____ percent

3. From related trade or business activities free from unrelated business income tax (UBIT):

SOURCE	ESTIMATED PROFIT	LIKELIHOOD OF RECEIPT
a. _____	$_____	_____ percent
b. _____	$_____	_____ percent
c. _____	$_____	_____ percent
d. _____	$_____	_____ percent
Subtotals:	$_____	_____ percent

4. From unrelated trade or business activities subject to UBIT:

SOURCE	ESTIMATED PROFIT	ESTIMATED UBIT	LIKELIHOOD OF RECEIPT
a. _____	$_____	$_____	_____ percent
b. _____	$_____	$_____	_____ percent
c. _____	$_____	$_____	_____ percent
d. _____	$_____	$_____	_____ percent
Subtotals:	$_____	$_____	_____ percent

5. From asset-generated income free from UBIT:

SOURCE	ESTIMATED PROFIT	LIKELIHOOD OF RECEIPT
a. _____	$_____	_____ percent
b. _____	$_____	_____ percent
c. _____	$_____	_____ percent
d. _____	$_____	_____ percent
Subtotals:	$_____	_____ percent

**EXHIBIT
15.1**   **Worksheet for Identifying Sources,
Types, and Amounts of Funds *(continued)***

6. From asset-generated income subject to UBIT:

SOURCE	ESTIMATED PROFIT	ESTIMATED UBIT	LIKELIHOOD OF RECEIPT
a._____	\$_____	\$_____	_____ percent
b._____	\$_____	\$_____	_____ percent
c._____	\$_____	\$_____	_____ percent
d._____	\$_____	\$_____	_____ percent
Subtotals:	\$_____	\$_____	_____ percent

7. From direct cash contributions (not pledges):

SOURCE	AMOUNT	LIKELIHOOD OF RECEIPT
a._____	\$_____	_____ percent
b._____	\$_____	_____ percent
c._____	\$_____	_____ percent
d._____	\$_____	_____ percent
Subtotals:	\$_____	_____ percent

8. From pledged cash contributions:

SOURCE	AMOUNT	LIKELIHOOD OF RECEIPT
a._____	\$_____	_____ percent
b._____	\$_____	_____ percent
c._____	\$_____	_____ percent
d._____	\$_____	_____ percent
Subtotals:	\$_____	_____ percent

9. From noncash (in-kind) contributions:

SOURCE AND NATURE OF CONTRIBUTION	ESTIMATED VALUE	LIKELIHOOD OF RECEIPT
a._____	\$_____	_____ percent
b._____	\$_____	_____ percent
c._____	\$_____	_____ percent
d._____	\$_____	_____ percent
Subtotals:	\$_____	_____ percent

	AMOUNT	LIKELIHOOD OF RECEIPT
Total of restricted funds:	\$_____	_____ percent

(You will need written descriptions
of all funding source restrictions.)

Total of unrestricted funds:	\$_____	_____ percent
Total estimated funds:	\$_____	_____ percent

EXHIBIT 15.2   Worksheet for Analyzing the Certainty of Future Income

Current Date: _____   Fiscal Year: _____ to _____

                                    (month/day/year)   (month/day/year)

1. Assured Income:

Source and Purpose	Amount	Percentage of Certainty	Include in Budget?
_____	_____	_____ percent	Yes No
_____	_____	_____ percent	Yes No
_____	_____	_____ percent	Yes No

Amount to Include in Budget: $_____

2. Likely Income But Not Assured:

Source and Purpose	Amount	Percentage of Certainty	Include in Budget?
_____	_____	_____ percent	Yes No
_____	_____	_____ percent	Yes No
_____	_____	_____ percent	Yes No

Amount to Include in Budget: $_____

3. Uncertain Income:

Source and Purpose	Amount	Percentage of Certainty	Include in Budget?
_____	_____	_____ percent	Yes No
_____	_____	_____ percent	Yes No
_____	_____	_____ percent	Yes No

Amount to Include in Budget: $_____

Total amount of income to include in budget: $_____
Amount of uncertain income included in above total: $_____
Total amount of uncertain income not included: $_____
Total amount of income possible in coming year: $_____
Total amount of income certain in coming year: $_____

1. Annual Policy Decisions

Decisions must be made on the following topics:

- Cost increases: Will salaries, wages, and operating expenses be increased? If so, by how much? (Make sure to include planned and contractual wage increases.)

- Costs of generating future income: If anticipated but as yet unsolicited income (funds to be sought during the coming year) is included in the budget, any additional expenses related to generating it should also be detailed. This can include additional costs of proposal writing, fundraising campaigns, and fundraising events.

2. Projecting Salaries and Wages

For most nonprofits, salaries and wages are the largest part of the annual operating budget, so they must be projected as accurately as possible. Failing to budget properly for equipment and other "discretionary expenses" often can be corrected by delaying purchases; failing to meet a payroll because of incorrect forecasting is far more serious. Carefully budgeting personnel costs reduces the chance of unanticipated financial difficulties during the fiscal year.

The simplest way to budget for salaries and wages is to create a spreadsheet listing all authorized positions, including vacant ones that will be filled. For each position listed, include the budgeted hourly rate, the budgeted total number of work hours, and the budgeted wages. If the position is salaried, include the total annual salary and then calculate the hourly rate by dividing the annual salary by the number of hours in a workweek, multiplied by 52 weeks.

Position listings should be maintained throughout the year, and any changes in authorized positions or hourly rates should be posted as they occur. In this way, the updated spreadsheet can be used for the next annual budgeting process. The spreadsheet can also be used to calculate the impact of any proposed salary, wage, or fringe benefit increases. By adding columns to the spreadsheet with formulas for calculating the effect of variables (such as percentage of salary increase and effective date), the total impact of an increase can be calculated rapidly and accurately.

Because nonprofits' payroll costs frequently constitute 60 to 85 percent of total expenses, it may be wise to do one of the two following things:

- Budget for overtime in a separate line item. If the entire overtime line-item amount is not used, it can be reassigned to cover deficits in other areas or used to build the organization's surplus (if allowed by the funding source).

- Budget for part-time staff in a separate line item. Rather than paying regular staff time-and-a-half or more for overtime, it may be more desirable to budget for and hire part-time staff to meet overtime demands.

3. Projecting Fringe Benefits

Ways to project employee fringe benefit costs vary according to the size of the nonprofit, applicable state and local laws affecting minimum benefits, and benefits offered and how they are provided. Use government publications to identify the employer's share of social security taxes, Medicare, and unemployment insurance for the coming year. Insurance carriers often can provide estimated increases in the cost of health, life, and workers' compensation insurance.

Pay particular attention to budgeting for workers' compensation insurance, including giving it its own line item. In some jurisdictions, insurance companies have more than one year to bill employers for workers' compensation claims they have paid out. If there have been a number of staff injuries, the organization may have to make large payments to maintain coverage. Specialized consultants can help review claims history and identify ways to reduce your workers' compensation expenses.

4. Projecting Other Operating Costs

Projecting operating costs beyond salaries and fringe benefits usually requires year-to-year adjustment for (1) any projected change in prices (usually increases) for goods and services and (2) any projected change in usage or volume of goods and services.

a. Identifying Projected Prices. Identify increases built into leases and other contracts. Then project price changes for services, supplies, materials, commodities, and equipment required to operate programs or activities. The simplest way is to contact vendors or providers of services and ask for estimates of any anticipated price changes. (This approach works best for vendors with which the organization has a long-standing relationship.) If vendors cannot or will not give price increase estimates, you must develop independent estimates.

Many nonprofits simply use the most recent estimated annual rate of inflation. Although this may not be accurate for each individual item or service to be purchased, it usually results in a sufficient across-the-board increase in the operating budget to cover most individual price increases.

When nonsalary costs are a substantial part of the operating budget, take particular care projecting price increases. For example, if printing and postage make up a large part of the annual budget, get accurate estimates of future costs from printers and paper vendors, and contact the postal service regarding possible postage increases.

b. Identifying Changes in Usage or Volume. The second step in projecting operating costs is to identify changes in operations likely to reduce or increase the use of supplies, materials, services, equipment, or other nonsalary costs. Changes can come from expanding or contracting existing programs or services, an increase or reduction in demand for existing programs or services, or the introduction of new programs or services. For example, expanding day care center enrollment six months into the new fiscal year will increase income and expenses. Similarly, plans to phase out a program during the first three-quarters of the next fiscal year require projecting when and by how much costs are likely to decrease.

Often both of the above steps are needed to project operating costs accurately. For example, if postage rates will increase by 10 percent beginning the fourth quarter of the next fiscal year (with no increase in the amount of mail to be sent), and half of anticipated mailings will occur after that date, one option is to increase the current postage budget by 5 percent. Another is to schedule more of the planned mailings before the increase takes effect.

C. Summarizing Proposed Changes in Draft Budgets

Exhibit 15.3 contains a sample form for summarizing proposed changes in draft budgets submitted for the CFO's, CEO's, or board's review and approval. Exhibit 15.4 contains a blank copy of the same form; it can be photocopied, modified, and used in the preparation of draft program, unit, or organizationwide budgets.

EXHIBIT 15.3   **Sample Form for Summarizing Proposed Draft Budget Changes**

Program/Unit: <u>Project Head Start</u>   Date Submitted: __ /__ /__ By: _____

Date Reviewed: __ /__ /__ Action Taken: _____ Date Acted On: __ /__ /__ By: _____

	FOR CURRENT YEAR		FOR NEXT YEAR'S BUDGET	
CHANGES IN BUDGET CATEGORIES	**BUDGETED AMOUNT**	**ESTIMATED ACTUAL AMOUNT**	**REQUESTED INCREASE (DECREASE)**	**APPROVED INCREASE (DECREASE)**
Salaries: Average 4 percent merit increase	_____	_____	_____	_____
1 additional teacher's aide	_____	_____	_____	_____
1 vacancy (part-time social worker)	_____	_____	_____	_____
Subtotal, Salaries:	_____	_____	_____	_____
Consultants and professional fees:	_____	_____	_____	_____
Subscriptions:	_____	_____	_____	_____
Classroom supplies:	_____	_____	_____	_____

EXHIBIT 15.4   **Blank Form for Summarizing Proposed Draft Budget Changes**

Program/Unit: _____   Date Submitted: __ /__ /__ By: _____

Date Reviewed: __ /__ /__ Action Taken: _____ Date Acted On: __ /__ /__ By: _____

	FOR CURRENT YEAR		FOR NEXT YEAR'S BUDGET	
CHANGES IN BUDGET CATEGORIES	**BUDGETED AMOUNT**	**ESTIMATED ACTUAL AMOUNT**	**REQUESTED INCREASE (DECREASE)**	**APPROVED INCREASE (DECREASE)**
	_____	_____	_____	_____
	_____	_____	_____	_____
	_____	_____	_____	_____
	_____	_____	_____	_____
	_____	_____	_____	_____
	_____	_____	_____	_____
	_____	_____	_____	_____

D. Budget Highlights

A budget should have a written summary of budget assumptions and highlights, explaining any significant proposed changes, any actions affecting personnel (new positions sought, positions recommended to be eliminated, proposed promotions or raises), and any other significant changes to the program's or unit's current budget or operations. Exhibit 15.5 shows a sample of a unit's budget assumptions and highlights.

EXHIBIT 15.5   **Example of One Unit's Budget Assumptions and Highlights**

Program or Unit: _Youth Department_

Program Director: _____   Date: _8/1/97_

Dear _Roger_ :

Total Income and Expenses

As the accompanying draft budget shows, next year's budgeted 1998 income for the Youth Department is projected to exceed budgeted expenses by $800, with expenses of $55,000 and income of $55,800. Following is a general summary of changes from this year's budget.

Income Highlights

In July of this year, the State Department of Youth Services informed us that our allocation for the coming year would be reduced by $5,000 due to cutbacks by the state legislature. To address this potential income shortfall, the proposed budget provides for holding a citywide 10K "Run for Youth" scheduled for fall next year, which is expected to generate $10,000 in additional contributions from individuals and corporate gifts.

Expense Highlights

The major increase in expenses reflects the 2 percent increase in salaries and wages for eligible employees (those hired on or before [eligibility date]). The scheduled 10K Run for Youth will increase printing, postage, and consulting expenses by $2,000.

Allocating Administrative, Overhead, and Shared Costs

Most nonprofits generate costs associated with administrative staff and operations that support more than one function within the nonprofit and are not directly attributable to specific programs or activities. Examples include salaries for senior management; central accounting and purchasing staff; shared facilities costs; and other activities, which benefit more than one program, unit, or cost center. Such costs may be assigned to individual program or unit budgets in appropriate percentages, or they may be listed in their own consolidated central budget.

Typically, administrative, overhead, and shared costs are allocated on some predetermined basis to the specific programs and activities they support. While this involves extra steps in budgeting and accounting for actual costs, the benefits justify the effort. First, allocating administrative and overhead costs produces a budget that accurately reflects the true costs of program operations. After allocation, program budgets include not only the direct costs of program staff, supplies, services, and equipment, but also a share of the cost of the central or shared services and facilities required for day-to-day operations. Moreover, if a program is eliminated, the administrative, overhead or shared costs that must be reallocated or reduced are clearly shown.

Second, allocating administrative and overhead costs may help increase reimbursement. Funding sources may be more willing to support the overhead or indirect costs of a program if the budget clearly shows that these costs are an integral part of the program to be funded.

A. Allocation Methods

The key to allocating administrative and overhead costs successfully is having a rational and justifiable written cost allocation plan. Some commonly used methods include distributing administrative and overhead costs based on a program's or unit's:

1. Percentage share of the total budget or the total salary budget

2. Per-unit cost of an activity

3. Use of space

All of these allocation methods may be used in a program or unit budget in the appropriate context. For example, when allocating administrative costs (such as costs for senior management, accounting, and purchasing), it may be appropriate to use the *percentage share of total budget* or *total salary budget* methods to allocate costs. When allocating shared rent and maintenance costs, a method based on the square footage used by programs is often more appropriate.

Specific allocation methods should be reasonable, applied consistently, and substantiated by the nonprofit's records. Following are some additional examples:

1. Personnel and consultant costs can be allocated based on employee and consultant time records that clearly identify time spent on specific projects or activities. Employees' and consultants' individual travel and other business expenses can be allocated on the same basis.

2. Fringe benefits can be allocated based on the percentage allocation of individual salaries.

3. Telephone expenses are most efficiently documented and allocated by having separate numbers for each department or activity, which allows the organization to request separate bills from the telephone company. Additionally, larger nonprofits may benefit from purchasing a software product that will automatically monitor telephone use by cost center.

4. Photocopying costs can be allocated based on a log that records the specific project for which photocopying is done. More sophisticated photocopiers have electronic logs that can track copies made for each department or project. Substantial copying volume may justify the use of a separate copying machine dedicated to a specific department.

5. Postage costs can also be allocated based on a log, in which postage use is recorded by specific project. High postage expenses may justify a separate postage meter for a specific department.

6. Space and facilities costs, including utilities and maintenance, can be allocated based on square footage or time in use.

7. Vehicle use should be allocated based on mileage recorded in a log that identifies the driver, round trip, mileage, purpose, and specific program or activity.

No matter which allocation method is used for a particular program or unit budget category, methods should be written down and applied uniformly to all similar budget development and accounting transactions. Documentation should be updated to reflect any changes in the method and maintained for use by staff and outside auditors. Additionally, allocation plans may be subject to funding source rules, adherence to which is ensured through allocation plan review and written approval by funding sources. Those developing allocation guidelines should review all funding source requirements before choosing allocation methods. Some sources require organizations to use designated allocation methods for allocating administrative, overhead, and shared costs.

B. Worksheet for Allocating Costs

Exhibit 16.1 contains a worksheet to use in identifying and allocating administrative, overhead, and shared costs.

EXHIBIT 16.1	Worksheet for Identifying and Allocating Administrative, Overhead, and Shared Costs

ALLOCABLE COSTS:	ALLOCATIONS					
	PROGRAM OR UNIT	PROGRAM OR UNIT	PROGRAM OR UNIT	PROGRAM OR UNIT	PROGRAM OR UNIT	TOTAL ALLOCATED

I. Personnel

A. Salaries and Wages
(list positions and basis for allocation)
Central administration:
Clerical:
Fiscal:
Human resources:
Public relations:
Other allocable positions:

B. Fringe Benefits (list positions)
Full time:
Part time:

C. Consultants and Contract or Professional Services
(list areas and basis of allocation)
Legal:
Accounting:
Auditing:
Medical:
Educational:
Psychiatric:
Psychological:
Total allocated personnel costs:

II. Other Than Personnel Costs

A. Consumable Materials and Supplies
(list items and basis for allocation)
Program supplies:
Vocational supplies:
Recreational supplies:
Laundry supplies:
Housekeeping supplies:
Office supplies:
Food and beverages:

B. Facilities
(describe basis of allocation)
Program administration:
Program services and activities:
Client residences:
Staff offices:

EXHIBIT 16.1   **Worksheet for Identifying and Allocating Administrative, Overhead, and Shared Costs** *(continued)*

ALLOCABLE COSTS:	PROGRAM OR UNIT	PROGRAM OR UNIT	PROGRAM OR UNIT	PROGRAM OR UNIT	PROGRAM OR UNIT	TOTAL ALLOCATED
C. Insurance Needed for Program Facilities (list items; describe basis of allocation)						
D. Direct Assistance to Clients (list items; describe basis of allocation)						
Allowances (Cash payments):						
Personal items:						
Other assistance:						
E. Travel and Transportation for Program Operations (describe basis of allocation)						
Transporting clients:						
Staff travel:						
Vehicles to be operated:						
Vehicle/travel insurance:						
F. Training, Conferences, and Meetings (describe basis for allocation)						
Staff and client training:						
Staff meetings and conferences:						
G. Membership Dues for Business, Professional, or Technical Organizations (include basis for allocation)						
H. Subscriptions to Professional Publications (include basis for allocation)						
I. Other Insurance (list kinds and basis for allocation)						
J. Miscellaneous Goods and Services Not Identified Earlier (list kinds and basis of allocation)						
Total allocations:						

Revising Draft Operating Budgets

After receiving and totaling detailed, written draft budgets from organizational units and functional areas, the nonprofit's CFO (or other person preparing a proposed operating budget for presentation to the board) often must make adjustments to produce a proposed budget. Such adjustments can include modifying estimated income or projected expenses.

A. Updating Fiscal Projections

The first step in adjusting draft budgets is to reexamine the assumptions used in projecting income and expenses. Several weeks or months may have elapsed since the original projections, and circumstances may have changed.

Obviously a time lapse can produce either good or bad news. Good news could include finding that actual price increases for goods and services are lower than originally estimated. Similarly, new income sources may have been found, or higher amounts of income than originally estimated may be available. Possible bad news could include new program or administrative requirements demanding greater expense than first estimated or potential income that has shrunk or disappeared entirely.

In any event, the person preparing the proposed operating budget must adjust income and expense figures to project the most accurate picture of the nonprofit's future financial position. This picture will help indicate what specific adjustments to draft budgets will be required.

Nonprofits can adjust budgets by modifying costs or income. To modify income, each nonprofit must do an analysis (including identifying any associated increases in costs) and develop its own strategy to ensure sufficient income. Cost modification approaches, on the other hand, tend to involve either trimming draft budgets in ways that will not significantly affect basic operations or making deeper cuts, which will.

B. Trimming Draft Budgets

There are ways to trim draft budgets that have little or no significant effect on programs and activities. Some ideas follow.

1. *Calculating salary increases as of anniversary dates.* Depending on the organization's personnel policies, union contracts, and other organizational policies, it may be possible to reduce salary and wage costs by calculating salary increases as of anniversary dates. This is done by scheduling the increases to occur on each employee's anniversary date of employment. Calculate each position's actual salary and benefits before the anniversary date at the old rate and after the anniversary date at the new rate.

2. *Using competitive bidding.* Having different vendors submit competitive written bids for commonly purchased goods and services (including insurance) can help reduce expenses. This is especially true when a particular item has never been put out for bid, or when an existing contract has not been rebid for several years.

3. *Analyzing the use of service agreements.* Explore the relative benefits of purchasing a service agreement for maintenance and repair of equipment versus paying maintenance and repair costs per occurrence. Similarly, determine if each existing service agreement is being used enough to justify its cost. Depending on the age and condition of equipment, changing the current approach could reduce costs.

4. *Seeking economies of scale in purchasing.* Examine current purchasing patterns and procedures to see if bundling purchases currently made separately might produce economies of scale and lower prices. In addition to internal bundling of purchases, explore the possibility of entering into mutually beneficial cooperative purchasing agreements with other nonprofits in the same geographic area.

5. *Analyzing administrative costs.* Consider consolidating or outsourcing administrative functions to reduce costs. For example, if the same or similar data processing functions are performed by staff in different units or programs, consolidating the functions may allow for a reduction in staff costs or overtime expenses. Outsourcing operations like payroll and check preparation may make it possible to save money through reducing staff. Moreover, outsourcing will free up staff to perform more critical functions, thus avoiding hiring additional people.

6. *Deferring or eliminating low-priority purchases.* Have the unit or program managers submitting draft budgets prioritize their requested purchases. Those responsible for preparing the organizationwide budget may then review the prioritized requests to determine which purchases may be postponed or eliminated.

C. When More and Deeper Cuts Are Needed

If the budget has been trimmed as far as possible yet further cuts are still required, a nonprofit may have to reduce expenses that will affect existing or proposed programs and activities. It is likely that deeper cuts will result in the nonprofit's compromising some aspect of the services it offers.

Obviously, whenever more extreme budget-cutting actions are necessary, program or unit managers should have a high degree of involvement in determining the cuts. For instance, they may identify possible reductions to their budgets and then rank the reductions from least damaging to most. This ranking will create guidelines for making sensible budget cuts that do the least damage from the perspective of program and unit leaders, who are most involved in day-to-day operations of the programs being modified.

Following are some additional options for significant cost cutting:

1. Postpone filling new or vacant positions.

2. Delay starting new activities or expanding existing ones (subject to any funding source requirements). The organization can thereby postpone hiring new personnel and defer new expenses for operating and equipment costs until a later date.

3. If a decision is made to eliminate a proposed new program, be sure to eliminate all expenses associated with it. New activities may have hidden costs in operating and capital budgets, which should be carefully reviewed to ensure that all appropriate accounts are reduced.

4. Reduce programs and services. Minor adjustments to service levels or a gradual downsizing of programs often can yield sufficient savings to balance the budget, while minimizing adverse impact on clients.

5. If cuts require reductions in existing staff positions, allow for the expenses connected with laying off people or terminating positions—for example, paying out any contractual or policy requirements, such as severance pay, buyout clauses, or continuation of fringe benefit coverage for a specified period.

D. Avoiding Potential Budget-Cutting Problems

Before cutting costs, those responsible for trimming or cutting budgets must become completely familiar with the exact nature and terms of all funding contracts and grant agreements to ensure their due consideration in budget-cutting decisions.

The terms of contracts and grant agreements are often subject to audit, so it is important to make sure that reducing expenses at the beginning of a program year will not create problems in the future. For instance, some contracts or grants may require that a nonprofit serve specific numbers of people or provide specified amounts of service within a given time period. Reducing staff or other expenses too sharply may leave the organization with insufficient resources to meet its obligations, and the audit may result in questioned costs that may have to be repaid.

Cutting expenses can backfire in other ways too, depending on the nature of the grant or contract. Reducing the total expenses involved in fee-for-service contracts will usually result in cost savings to the organization. However, when it comes to cost-reimbursement contracts, reducing expenses can actually reduce the total amount of reimbursement an organization is eligible to receive. Thus, careful review of all applicable contracts and grant agreements is essential before cutting program costs.

Presenting Your Annual Budget Proposal to the Board

Once draft budgets have been analyzed, modified, and balanced, and any necessary technical adjustments have been made, it is time to prepare an overall budget document. This document will be used to present the proposed budget first to the board and then to any other interested parties, such as managers, staff, clients, the press, and the general public. The following subsections describe basic elements of a budget presentation document with illustrative examples.

A. Letter of Transmittal

A letter of transmittal acts as the cover letter for the budget document. Generally it is written by the CEO to the board, although in some cases the CFO may write it. The letter of transmittal should contain at least two summaries:

1. A summary of the policies, goals, and objectives that guided the development of the budget

2. A summary of the total income and expenses contained in the budget

Many transmittal letters also contain brief summaries of major budget highlights, such as new programs or initiatives, or changes to existing activities. When large, complex budgets are being submitted, the letter of transmittal may be the only part of the budget that members of the board, the press, and the general public read thoroughly. Because the letter is likely to shape board decisions, as well as any media stories and public perceptions, it should contain all pertinent information and should be written clearly and concisely.

Exhibit 18.1 contains an example of a letter of transmittal to the board. (This letter may also be used in a modified form by program managers to introduce program and unit budgets to the CEO and CFO.)

B. Total, Organizationwide Budget Summary

A total organizationwide budget summary offers an at-a-glance version of the budget and tends to be a primary source of information for board members and the media. There should be summaries of all income and expenses, including (at a minimum):

EXHIBIT 18.1 **Sample Letter of Transmittal**

November 30, 1998

Board of Trustees
XYZ Services, Incorporated

Ladies and Gentlemen:

I am pleased to present XYZ Services' proposed 1999 budget, which was developed in accordance with the fiscal policies and program priorities set by the Board at its strategic planning sessions last September. Specifically, these policies and procedures were:

- To balance the budget without using cash reserves;
- To budget a 2 percent salary and wage increase for eligible employees, effective January 1, 1999;
- To keep programs and services at existing levels;
- To expand fundraising to ensure support for all activities and needed administrative capabilities;
- To keep increases in client fees below inflation.

As the accompanying financial schedules indicate, budgeted 1999 income will exceed budgeted expenses by $1,600, with expenses of $855,000 and income of $856,600. Following is a general summary of changes from last year's budget.

Income Highlights: Shortly after the strategic planning sessions, the United Way informed us that our allocation for fiscal 1999 would be reduced by $23,000 due to lower contribution levels and recent decisions by the United Way resource allocation committee. To address this potential income shortfall, the proposed budget provides for expanded fundraising activities, including a special event to be scheduled for Fall 1999 and an additional direct mail solicitation immediately following the event. These activities are expected to generate $30,000 in additional contributions from individuals, plus a small increase in corporate gifts.

The proposed budget for 1999 includes a moderate fee increase for day care services. Because of this and an expanded enrollment, day care income is expected to increase by a total of 5.4 percent, with no more than a 2 percent increase in fees. The budget contains no other fee increases.

Expense Highlights: The major increase in expenses reflects the 2 percent increase in salaries and wages for eligible employees. For the second consecutive year, we have negotiated a favorable rate for health and life insurance benefits, resulting in no increase in the average rate used to calculate their cost. However, these rates are expected to rise significantly in the 2000 budget. The expanded fundraising efforts scheduled for Fall 1999 will increase overall printing, postage, and consulting expenses.

On behalf of the staff of XYZ Services, I would like to thank all Board members for their leadership and direction in developing this proposed budget. We look forward to reviewing it with you and providing any information or clarification you may need before its final approval.

Yours truly,

(Signature of CEO and/or CFO)

1. A summary of income by individual sources.

2. A summary of expenses by broad categories, such as salaries and wages, consultants and contract services, supplies, facilities, materials, and equipment. For an example of an expense budget summary appropriate to submit for board review, see Exhibit 18.2.

The overall budget summary may also include summaries of comparative data for each of the past three years to let the reader understand any changes in income, income sources, expenses, and kinds of expenses that may have occurred. The summary should also contain a column indicating the total change (expressed as a percentage or a dollar amount) from the previous year's budget.

C. Program, Unit, or Activity Budget Summaries

It is desirable for nonprofits with multiple programs and services to summarize categories of income and expenses by individual program or unit as well. This program or unit budget summary is simply another way of presenting overall income and expense information and helps illustrate priorities for the coming year. Ideally, a program or unit budget summary includes the following items:

1. A statement of purpose for the program

2. The program or unit's goals and objectives for the budget year

3. A summary of program income and expenses, along with historical comparison data from prior years

4. A brief narrative summary of major changes from the prior year's budget

For an example of a program or unit budget summary, see Resource B.

D. Detailed, Organizationwide Line-Item Expense Budget

Proposed budget documents should also include projected expenses by individual line item or account. In general, line-item budgets serve three useful purposes:

1. They present in detail exactly what the budget contains.

2. After the budget is approved, they give managers an exact indication of the resources available and the income they are expected to generate.

3. The line-item detail of the approved budget is then entered into the accounting system and provides the basis for tracking, controlling, and reporting budgeted versus actual income and expenses during the coming year.

Smaller nonprofits may provide needed line-item detail in a single listing of all the expense accounts. Larger nonprofits with multiple programs may find it useful to provide similar line-item expense detail for each individual program or activity as well. For an example of a detailed, line-item expense budget, see Resource E.

EXHIBIT 18.2 ABC Corporation Summary Expense Budget for Board Review

CATEGORIES	CHILD CARE	COMMUNITY SERVICES	BASIC NEEDS	EXECUTIVE OFFICE	HOUSING	ADMINISTRATIVE SERVICES	RESEARCH	MEDICAL/ DENTAL	INFORMATION/ EVALUATION	TOTALS
Personnel	$254,130	$41,600	$82,253	$93,835	$31,085	$49,385	$122,920	$1,000	$36,910	$713,118
Fringe Benefits	68,615	11,230	22,208	25,335	8,395	13,335	33,190	270	9,965	192,543
Repairs					85,000					85,000
Utility Cost (Space/Rental)	2,000		2,000		10,620	2,810		3,000		20,430
Automatic Data Processing	675		125	135	45	126	225			1,331
Legal				5,000				100		5,100
Audit	1,300	100	100	1,000	320			500		3,320
Staff/Board Development	500	200	250	2,000	200	200	1,000		200	4,550
Vehicle, Fuel, Maintenance			5,000	2,000						7,000
Local Travel	250	200	500		500	500	100		100	2,150
Out-of-Town Travel			200	2,000			1,500		500	4,200
Desktop Supplies		300	500	1,500		150	640		250	3,340
Space Costs and Rental	15,455	1,130	12,000	5,610	1,130	2,260	5,605	13,105		56,295
Classroom Supplies	2,000									2,000
Client or Pupil Supplies		1,000								1,000
Maintenance Supplies	40	40	500	60	800		160	100		1,660
Reproduction Supplies	1,340		800	1,000	200	400	500		200	4,440
Project Supplies	100	40	200							340
Printing and Reproduction		1,700	2,000				500			4,200

EXHIBIT 18.2 ABC Corporation Summary Expense Budget for Board Review (continued)

Categories	Child Care	Community Services	Basic Needs	Executive Office	Housing	Administrative Services	Research	Medical/ Dental	Information/ Evaluation	Totals
Maintenance and Upkeep	500				1,000		60			1,560
Telephone	500	800	2,600	1,200	400		1,200	100	300	7,100
Postage		2,500	1,000	2,000			1,000		200	6,700
Computer Equipment			2,000	1,500			2,000		500	6,000
Equipment Service Agreement		700	1,600	1,000	700	9,900	1,000	11,485		26,385
Vehicle Insurance			500	1,500						2,000
Publications/ Subscriptions		25		200			200		500	925
Liability Insurance	7,855	300	1,740	210	785		210	1,245		12,345
Food Costs		500								500
Improvements			20,000			7,200		7,200		34,400
Consultants						1,500	3,000	2,000		6,500
Vehicle Operating Expenses										0
Field Trips										0
Equipment Maintenance and Repair	200					30,000		2,940		33,140
Other Child Services										0
Lease				5,000						5,000
Fiscal Accounting										0
Moving Expenses		600		900	300	900	1,500		300	4,500
Contingency								2,500		2,500
Miscellaneous			6,000					3,600		9,600
TOTALS:	$355,420	$62,965	$164,076	$152,985	$141,480	$118,666	$176,510	$49,145	$49,925	$1,271,172

E. Individual Program or Unit Budgets

Detailed, line-item budgets for each individual program, activity, or unit are particularly useful for nonprofits that have several programs or units with substantially different purposes, operations, or funding sources. Individual line-item budgets for each program or unit should highlight major fiscal and programmatic changes, thus enabling the reader to understand fully the implications for the specific program or service provided.

See Resource B for an example of an individual program or unit budget.

F. Other Useful Information

The budget presentation document may include separate sections or appendixes providing additional information, such as:

1. A glossary of terms if the proposed budget document uses unfamiliar, technical language

2. A summary of major financial and budget policies reflected in the proposed budget, including a description and schedule of the budgeting process; a summary description of specific budgeting assumptions, guidelines, and goals; and other information for understanding the basis for the budget

3. A summary of strategic (long-range) organizational goals and objectives, defined by the board, which guide the organization's long- and short-term financial planning

4. A table of organization structure showing staffing levels by organizational units

5. Graphics depicting key items of information, such as a pie chart that shows expenses allocated by program area; bar charts indicating changes in expenses or income over several years; and other types of graphics showing demand and service levels over time

CHAPTER 19 Board Review, Revision, and Approval of the Final Budget

Board members, because of their varied backgrounds, have the potential to make valuable contributions to the budgeting process. In order to achieve this potential, board members must take the time to develop an understanding of all the aspects of budgeting.

Board review of proposed budgets might be structured in a number of ways. During the original planning and policy development process, top management and the board should determine the board's specific roles and responsibilities. Some boards set aside a specific number of hours or meetings to allow the board as a whole to review, revise, and approve proposed budgets. Others form working subcommittees to review the various proposed budgets and report back to the entire board. In addition, the board may involve the organization's independent auditors or other outside resource people to help review proposed budgets.

Obviously, the more thorough the board review is, the more time it requires. The budget team then needs enough time to consider the board's concerns, make appropriate revisions, and send the budget back for another review cycle before final budget approval.

Exhibits 19.1 and 19.2 are useful for planning and conducting the budget review.

EXHIBIT 19.1 **Worksheet for Preparing for Board Review of Proposed Budget**

1. The proposed budget will be reviewed by:

   ☐ The board as a whole.

   ☐ One or more board committees (name the committees): _____.

   ☐ Some other group (describe its composition): _____.

   ☐ Not yet decided (identify who will decide and when): _____.

2. If not all board members will be invited to participate, name those who will:

   _____   _____   _____

   _____   _____   _____

   _____   _____   _____

   _____   _____   _____

EXHIBIT 19.1 **Worksheet for Preparing for Board Review of Proposed Budget** *(continued)*

3. When and where will they review the budget?

   Date: ____ /____ /____   Time: _____   Place: _____

4. By what date before the review meeting will they receive copies of the proposed budget?

   _____

5. What persons other than board members will attend the budget review meeting?

   _____   _____   _____

   _____   _____   _____

   _____   _____   _____

6. Who is responsible for making sure items 1 through 5 take place? _____

   _____

7. Who will moderate the board budget review meeting? _____

   _____

8. Who will set review ground rules and present the proposed budget? _____

   _____

9. Who will compile written board review results and recommendations? _____

   _____

10. To whom will board review results be reported? _____

    _____

11. What additional materials will the board need to conduct its review? Who will make sure needed materials are available?

    MATERIALS NEEDED   PERSON(S) RESPONSIBLE

    _____   _____

    _____   _____

    _____   _____

    _____   _____

12. How will any differences between the board and management be addressed? _____

    _____

    _____

EXHIBIT 19.2   **Checklist for Board Review of Proposed Budget**

1. Make sure the budget is complete and accurate and has no typographical errors or mistakes in computation.

2. Ensure that the budget appears to reflect the organization's overall mission, strategic goals, and best use of its resources.
   - Carefully examine budgets and the programs, units, and activities they support to see how well they conform to the organization's purpose and objectives.
   - Determine if the allocation of resources to various programs and units is logical in relationship to the organization's priorities.

3. Determine how well the current year's actual financial performance to date matches last year's budget projections.
   - If actual income and expenses differ widely from those budgeted, determine why.
   - Decide how to make the proposed budget more accurate, to implement the approved budget more effectively, or both.

4. Decide if the proposed budget makes sense in the light of actual financial performance for the current year to date.
   - If individual programs or units are over budget, identify them and the specific cost categories and line items affected.
   - Determine what caused them to go over budget.
   - Find out what corrective action, if any, has been taken to help reduce the chance of going over budget again next year.
   - If actual income received has been less than the amount budgeted, identify the areas affected.
   - Determine what caused the reduced income.
   - Find out what corrective action, if any, has been taken to help reduce the chance of going over budget again next year.

5. Determine if budget variance analyses are regularly prepared and reviewed by program and unit heads, the CFO, CEO, and the board in order to catch potential income and expense problems before they become serious.
   - If budget variance analyses are not regularly prepared and reviewed, act to incorporate these steps into the process.

6. Decide if specific budget items are logical, in the sense that they represent the best way to carry out a program or unit's activities—for instance:
   - Examine issues of leasing versus purchasing.
   - See if resources can be shared between programs or units.
   - Determine if economies of scale through common purchasing would reduce purchasing costs.
   - Determine if needed services, such as payroll preparation, may be outsourced for a savings over hiring additional staff.

EXHIBIT 19.2   **Checklist for Board Review of Proposed Budget *(continued)***

7. **Be sure that each proposed budget meets the requirements of internal policies and procedures, specific funding sources, individual contracts and grant agreements, various accounting rules, and regulatory bodies such as the Internal Revenue Service.**

   - To carry out this "big picture" part of budget review, the board must understand and apply a wide range of requirements. (See the organization's independent auditor for help with this.)

8. **Overall, decide whether the organization possesses the talent, skills, and capability needed to implement the proposed programs and activities.**

   - If additional skills or knowledge are likely to be needed, determine what plans, if any, have been made to acquire them.

9. **If at all possible, make sure the total organizationwide budget includes designated reserve funds the organization can access if revenue projections fail, unforeseeable expenses arise, or unexpected opportunities present themselves.**

   - If no reserve funds are included, have the board address this issue, and set a goal of creating a specified reserve amount over the next two or three years.*

   *One method for addressing this issue that has proved successful for some nonprofits is to create an additional "contingency" budget category for several or all units, departments, or programs in the budget. "Contingency" should have 5 to 10 percent of the total program or unit budget amount set aside in it, which will be used to cover unexpected overexpenses or revenue shortfalls in the coming year. If it turns out at the end of the budgeted period that revenue and expense projections were accurate and actual performance shows no need for the contingency, unrestricted contingency funds may be used for staff bonuses or an additional contribution to a pension plan, or it may be saved for a rainy day or a good opportunity.

CHAPTER 20

Monitoring and Modifying Approved Budgets

When used in conjunction with financial reports, approved budgets form the basis for an effective performance-monitoring system. An organization's top and middle managers may compare approved budgets to actual financial reports to assess progress and monitor expenses. Regular comparisons will also help managers to identify income shortfalls, expenses overruns, or operational problems early enough to take corrective action.

A. Regular Financial Reporting and Monitoring

Program and unit managers should receive monthly reports on actual versus budgeted expenses and income for their areas of responsibility. These reports should identify variances from the budget. The program or unit manager should be asked to explain any differences beyond a specified percentage.

The CFO is responsible for ensuring that such reports are prepared as part of regular monitoring and evaluating the nonprofit's overall financial and operational position. The CFO must also prepare organizationwide financial reports, which are distributed to the CEO and the board for review and to determine if any follow-up action is required. The CFO's review of individual program or unit financial reports should include follow-up with the responsible program or unit manager, as well as bringing problems to the CEO's or the board's attention as needed.

Resource C contains a variety of examples of actual versus budgeted reports on income and expenses, and Resource D provides tools for analyzing financial reports, examining budgeted versus actual variances, and planning corrective action.

B. Planning and Taking Corrective Action

The CFO and program and unit managers should work closely together to identify potential or emerging financial problems and develop action plans for correcting them. If variances from budgeted figures are identified early enough, relatively mild corrective action may be all that is needed—for example, postponing filling new or vacant positions, deferring nonessential purchases, increasing fees charged for services, looking for alternative sources of revenue, or restricting travel, training, or payment of membership dues. If budgeted-to-actual variance is large or is discovered late in the fiscal year, more severe action may be required, such as a complete or partial freeze on hiring or purchasing (or both), delaying or reducing implementation of programs or services, or even staff layoffs.

It is important to act immediately when potential variances from budgeted income or expenses are found. Most problems only worsen over time, and delays in resolving them can lead to serious deficits, operational problems, and potential difficulties with funding sources and clients.

C. Modifying Budgets

No budget can accurately predict all the circumstances that may affect a nonprofit. That is why it is important to develop and document policies and procedures for modifying the approved budget, both in-house and with external funding sources. Explicit policies and procedures will provide the flexibility needed to respond to changing circumstances, while also maintaining proper financial controls.

1. Reasons for Modifying an Approved Budget

The organizationwide operating budget may contain income and expense estimates for an anticipated program that is never actually funded. The program's estimated income and expenses should be removed from the budget so that expenses will not be incurred without offsetting income.

Conversely, funding for a new program may be acquired during the year, requiring budget modifications to include the program's income and expenses.

Finally, unanticipated changes in personnel or operations may require reallocating funds between categories or line items within a budget. For example, if functions previously handled by employees are contracted out, the budget should be modified by transferring funds from its salary and wage account to its contract services account. Any obsolete staff positions should then be deleted from the budget.

2. Creating Written Budget Modification Policies and Procedures

Policies and procedures for modifying budgets should be composed and distributed to all employees with program, unit, fiscal, or budgetary management responsibilities. Grant- or contract-funded programs frequently contain funding source restrictions on making budget modifications and often require the nonprofit to obtain advance written approval from the funding source. Include the need to comply with any such specific funding source requirements in the document describing budget modification policies and procedures. In addition, make sure such policies and procedures contain the following components:

1. *Preferred timing for in-house budget modifications.* Allowing requests for in-house budget modifications at any time can lead to confusion. Nonprofits may restrict the frequency and timing of internal budget modification requests, except for emergencies or major problems. Internal requests for routine modifications might be considered

on a monthly, quarterly, or semiannual basis depending on the size and nature of the nonprofit's operations.

2. *Format for requesting in-house budget modifications.* Budget modification requests should specify the account and line item to be modified, the dollar amount of the requested modification, and a brief rationale for the modification. Exhibit 20.1 contains a sample form for requesting budget modifications.

3. *Reviewing budget modification requests.* Modification policies and procedures should clearly identify who is responsible for reviewing budget modification requests to ensure compliance with overall objectives, board policies and procedures, and any funding source requirements. Generally, budget modifications should not be used to establish expenses for a program, unit, or activity not previously approved by the board. In addition, each modification request should be reviewed to make sure that funds are available for transfer from one account or line item to another and that requests that would increase income and expenses are documented to ensure that income will actually be available.

4. *Approval authority for budget modifications.* To ensure clarity and proper accountability, clearly identify in writing who has the authority to approve budget modifications. Some nonprofits designate approval authority based on the type of modification. For example, if the modification does not affect policy or programs, the approval authority may be at the program or unit manager level, with CFO or CEO review. Modifications that have policy or program implications may require board action. In addition, funding sources frequently stipulate advance written approval (by the funding source) for any budget modifications.

EXHIBIT 20.1   **Form for Requesting Budget Modifications for Current Fiscal Year**

Program or Unit: _____   Date Submitted: ____ /____ /____   By: _____

Date Reviewed: ____ /____ /____   Action Taken: ____   Date Acted On: ____ /____ /____   By: _____

		FOR CURRENT BUDGET	
REQUESTED MODIFICATION AND EXPLANATION	FUNDING SOURCE(S)	REQUESTED INCREASE (DECREASE)	APPROVED INCREASE (DECREASE)
_____	_____	_____	_____
_____	_____	_____	_____
_____	_____	_____	_____
_____	_____	_____	_____
_____	_____	_____	_____
_____	_____	_____	_____
_____	_____	_____	_____

5. *Responsibility for follow-through.* In addition to approval authority, budget modification policies and procedures should define the person responsible for following through on modification requests. This includes informing program managers of final decisions about modification requests and making sure necessary changes are made to the financial management and reporting systems.

D. Cash Flow Projections and Planning

Cash flow refers to the relationship between the amount of cash an organization actually has available in the bank during a given period and the amount it needs to pay its bills during the same period. If there is more cash than there are bills, a nonprofit's cash flow is considered *positive*; if more must be paid out than is on hand, there is *negative* cash flow. Cash flow projections predict when cash will be received each month and compare the amount of cash expected with the amount of anticipated cash expenditures.

Doing regular cash flow projections is as important to nonprofits as fundraising and operations budgeting are. Effective cash flow management requires regular ongoing attention—not just attention when cash flow problems develop. Otherwise, one day there might not be enough cash in the bank to pay bills or salaries. The board and top management must identify projected periods of negative cash flow and plan specific actions to avoid shortfalls, so programs and services can continue without interruption. Exhibit 20.2 shows a simple cash flow budget for a small nonprofit.

EXHIBIT 20.2   Sample Cash Flow Budget for a Six-Month Period

	ANNUAL BUDGET[a]	MONTH					
		JANUARY	FEBRUARY	MARCH	APRIL	MAY	JUNE
Grants	$320,000	$50,000	$0	$75,000	$0	$0	$75,000
Contributions (fundraising)	150,000	0	0	0	0	0	75,000
Dues	70,000	35,000	15,000	10,000	1,000	1,000	1,000
	$540,000	85,000	15,000	85,000	1,000	1,000	151,000
Payroll	$360,000	30,000	30,000	30,000	30,000	30,000	30,000
Consultants	50,000	8,000	3,000	2,500	3,500	2,000	3,000
Space rental	30,000	1,500	2,000	1,500	2,500	1,500	1,500
Equipment	100,000	5,000	25,000	5,000	5,000	10,000	5,000
	$540,000	44,500	60,000	39,000	41,000	43,500	39,500
Cash surplus (deficit)		$40,500	$(45,000)	$46,000	$(40,000)	$(42,500)	$111,500
Cash balances at end of month		$40,500	$(4,500)	$41,500	$1,500	$(41,000)	$70,500

[a]Assumption is that opening cash is $0.

1. Causes of Cash Flow Problems

Having a cash flow problem does not necessarily mean that a nonprofit is operating at a deficit (although this could be the case). Nonprofit cash flow problems frequently are caused when income is received later than it is needed, typically in one of the following situations:

1. *After-the-fact funding.* Some grants or contracts reimburse the organization only after the fact (sometimes long after the fact) for rendering specific services; nevertheless, the nonprofit has to pay for staff, office space, equipment, supplies, and other resources in advance.

2. *Approval coming late.* Funding sources can approve existing programs for funding for the coming year weeks after the previous year's funding has ended.

3. *Cash coming late.* Funding sources may approve funding for a specific program to begin on a certain date, but not get around to providing the necessary cash until weeks or even months later.

To deal with problems like these, nonprofits must project and plan for adequate cash flow to meet regular expense obligations.

2. Cash Flow Projections and Planning

Many nonprofits find that it is most effective to do cash flow projections for the coming fiscal year in its entirety and then to update monthly projections throughout the year. Monthly cash flow projections focus on the anticipated timing of cash receipts and disbursements, highlighting times when cash flow problems are likely to occur or when idle cash that can be invested is likely to be available. It is important in both yearly and monthly projections to make note of any months in which expenditures and receipts are nearly identical. Negative cash flow can occur at these times, since actual expenditures and receipts will fluctuate somewhat from the estimates.

Management and the board should plan far enough in advance of potential problem periods to allow for action to offset negative cash flow. Board discussions and decisions regarding cash flow problems should be reflected in meeting minutes, along with information on those responsible for carrying out board decisions and any follow-up reports required.

3. Addressing Cash Shortfalls

During months when negative cash flow is expected, nonprofits need to generate more cash, reduce cash outlays, or both. For instance, a projection may show that cash shortages are projected for the second and fifth months of the fiscal year. To compensate for this problem, expenditures from the first month on might be postponed while receipt of revenue is accelerated. Potential options for addressing cash flow problems may include the following:

1. Postponing major purchases, hiring new staff, or instituting wage increases

2. Establishing payment schedules (installments) for costly items

3. Moving up the date of planned fundraising events

4. Planning additional ways of generating funds

5. Transferring funds from reserve accounts (if available and allowable under the rules governing these funds)

6. Seeking cash advances from funding organizations

7. Short-term borrowing

8. Actually reducing expenses (not just cash outlays)

4. Some Possible Drawbacks

The options listed for addressing cash shortfalls may have potential negative consequences. For instance, loans require interest payments, as do major purchases that are acquired though installment payments. Postponing payments to vendors without their agreement may generate ill will and possible loss of credit (or denial of vendor services) in the future. Furthermore, caution must always be used when transferring funds from internal accounts to avoid violating laws or contract obligations, especially when dealing with governmental or other restricted funds.

Making major cost reductions is difficult at best, but is fiscally responsible when no other viable alternative exists. In order to avoid loss of confidence among service recipients and funding sources, however, caution must be taken when reducing expenses. Once an organization has made major cuts in services, it runs the risk of earning a reputation for poor financial management. Nonprofits considering significantly reducing operations should discuss this with major funding sources to receive advice on other possible options.

21 Conclusion

Budgeting for nonprofits should be dynamic, collaborative, creative, and appropriately respected. When budgeting is regarded in this way, the product *and* the process will be of equal benefit to your organization. By going through a systematic, cooperative, and integrated budgeting effort, your organization reaps the rewards of improved coordination and communication. These elements will undoubtedly increase productivity and promote more effective problem solving. When the entire budgeting team operates from these perspectives, it is likely that the final product will serve the organization in many ways: as a monitoring tool, a planning tool, and a management tool.

Budgeting is both a means to an end and an end in itself. The goal should not be simply to develop a well-conceived document named "budget" that is either blindly adhered to or neglected in a file cabinet. Budgets should be consulted and monitored on a regular basis and modified when necessary. If it becomes clear as the budget year unfolds that the budget is not fulfilling its objectives, do not hesitate to modify it. Today's volatile economic and political landscape demands flexibility in budgeting for successful organizations. Continuing to execute a plan that no longer works, simply because it is "an approved budget," will not serve your organization's best interests.

Budgeting—effective budgeting, at least—is a process, a system, and an activity. Effective budgeting allows nonprofit organizations to employ limited resources better to meet their goals, as well as help the people and causes they serve. By developing and implementing a systematic budget and financial monitoring process, a nonprofit will make substantial strides toward fulfilling its mission.

An effective budgeting process also can provide an opportunity for people both inside and outside the organization to have a voice in determining how available funds and human resources are used. An effective budget and budget process are road maps that help guide everyone affiliated with the organization toward meeting its goals and objectives.

Budgeting should emphasize and enhance your organization's strengths. The annual goal-setting and budgeting process presents an excellent opportunity to review the organization's successes and failures in all aspects of its operations. As well, the annual budgeting process provides an excellent opportunity to identify activities and programs that have been unexpected successes. Such surprises often represent key guideposts for future action.

As you develop your organization's budget, keep the following concepts in mind to guide the overall process:

1. Good budgets are truthful and accurate and in alignment with the mission statement and strategic goals of the organization.

2. Good budgets are collaborative and are prepared based on good historical financial information and good research.

3. Budgets should be adhered to, but they also should be modified when necessary.

4. Good budgeting can become a basis for better understanding and cooperation within the entire organization.

5. Good budgeting is not easy, but it is your best chance for success.

We hope *The Budget Building Book for Nonprofits* is proving to be a valuable tool for you, whether you are using it to get information on specific topics or to put in place a new budgeting system or revamp an existing one.

PART THREE

Practical Budgeting Resources

Blank Master for Creating a Program or Unit Work Plan

To create a program or unit work plan, perform the following actions:

1. Photocopy the Blank Master for Creating a Program or Unit Work Plan (Exhibit A.1).

2. Using the photocopy, tailor the phases and action steps to meet your specific program or unit goals.

3. Under "Responsibility," identify those who are responsible for each phase and action step.

4. Under "Target Date," fill in the planned ending date for each step ("Week 1," "Month 1," "Months 1 to 3," and so forth).

5. Make sure that the finished work plan, if implemented, will reach the specific program or unit activity and outcome or goals.

EXHIBIT A.1   **Blank Master for Creating a Program or Unit Work Plan**

Some Tips on Creating a Program or Unit Work Plan

1. Items followed by a [P] may be relevant when creating a program or unit work plan.

2. Items without a [P] after them must be taken into account in planning programs, but probably are inappropriate for inclusion in a program or unit work plan being submitted to a funding source as part of a proposal.

3. In assigning responsibilities, more than one person may be identified.

4. In selecting target dates, allow for realities (like weather or getting staff on board and up to speed).

5. Remember that when you prepare a program or unit work plan someone else will be responsible for carrying out, it is important to be specific, detailed, and realistic. (Of course, the same is true if you are preparing a work plan that you will have to implement.)

EXHIBIT A.1	**Blank Master for Creating a Program or Unit Work Plan** *(continued)*

PROJECT PHASES AND ACTION STEPS	RESPONSIBILITY	TARGET DATE
A. Receive Official Funding Approval Notification		
1. Review the award notice or contract carefully to ensure understanding of all conditions of award. [P]		
2. After grant is received, prepare and place ads and recruit applicants for program or unit head. [P]		
3. Prepare and place ads and recruit applicants for program or unit staff. [P]		
4. Finalize job descriptions.		
B. Recruit, Interview, and Hire Staff		
1. Select interview team members, including representatives of key stakeholders. [P]		
2. Screen applications. [P]		
3. Schedule interviews and contact applicants. [P]		
4. Conduct interviews and select person(s) to hire. [P]		
5. Make offer to hire, negotiate as needed, and hire. [P]		
C. Orient Newly Hired People		
1. Send letter of hire.		
2. Schedule and conduct orientation meetings for newly hired people. [P]		
3. Have program or unit head establish contact with appropriate funding source representatives if not involved in the grant application process.		
4. Identify and subscribe to relevant publications.		
D. Staff Training and Development		
1. Design, schedule, conduct, and evaluate any needed staff training.		
2. Include staff of other programs as needed to support cross-training and collaboration.		
E. Facilities, Equipment, and Supplies		
1. Follow all bidding requirements and procurement policies and procedures. [P]		
2. Identify amount of funds available.		
3. Identify potential vendors. [P]		
4. Purchase needed equipment and supplies. [P]		
5. Seek satisfactory facilities. [P]		
6. Negotiate with potential landlords. [P]		
7. Agree on terms and sign leases. [P]		
F. Intra-Agency Linkages and Working Relationships		
1. Identify other relevant in-house programs and activities. [P]		
2. Review program goals, objectives, and design with their staff. [P]		

EXHIBIT A.1	Blank Master for Creating a Program or Unit Work Plan *(continued)*

PROJECT PHASES AND ACTION STEPS	RESPONSIBILITY	TARGET DATE
3. Determine mutual interests, functions, and roles. [P]		
4. Plan and negotiate linkages and procedures. [P]		
5. Create referral and collaboration procedures and forms. [P]		
6. Create written record of agreed-on roles, linkages, and procedures. [P]		
G. Interagency Linkages and Working Relationships		
1. Identify relevant outside agencies, programs, and activities. [P]		
2. Initiate contact and review program goals, objectives, and design with them. [P]		
3. Determine mutual interests, functions, and roles. [P]		
4. Form advisory or coordinating groups. [P]		
5. Plan and negotiate linkages and collaboration. [P]		
6. Create referral and collaboration procedures and forms. [P]		
7. Confirm with letters to create written record of agreed-on roles, linkages, and procedures. [P]		
8. Identify other relevant organizations and meetings to join and attend. [P]		
9. Identify in-house persons to maintain ongoing liaison with collaborating agency higher-ups. [P]		
10. Identify in-house persons to maintain liaison with collaborating agency program or service representatives. [P]		
H. Develop Evaluation Designs and Materials		
1. Identify funding source evaluation requirements. [P]		
2. Identify in-house evaluation requirements.		
3. Assign evaluation data-gathering and analysis responsibilities. [P]		
4. Identify evaluation standards for each goal and objective. [P]		
5. Identify evaluation methods for each goal and objective. [P]		
6. Identify evaluation data sources for each goal and objective. [P]		
7. Develop needed evaluation materials. [P]		
8. Create evaluation procedures and forms as needed. [P]		
9. Integrate data collection and evaluation requirements with any existing database capabilities. [P]		
10. Familiarize staff with program and financial evaluation requirements, procedures, forms, and responsibilities. [P]		
I. Record Keeping and Reporting		
1. Identify funding source reporting requirements. [P]		
2. Identify in-house reporting requirements.		
3. Assign data-gathering and reporting responsibilities. [P]		
4. Create or revise record-keeping forms, procedures, and responsibilities as needed. [P]		

EXHIBIT A.1 **Blank Master for Creating a Program or Unit Work Plan** *(continued)*

PROJECT PHASES AND ACTION STEPS	RESPONSIBILITY	TARGET DATE
5. Integrate data collection and record-keeping requirements with any existing database capabilities. [P]		
6. Familiarize staff with record-keeping and reporting forms, procedures, and responsibilities. [P]		
7. Begin data collection and analysis. [P]		
8. Prepare and submit required monthly in-house reports.		
9. Prepare and submit funding source reports and others as required (please specify report nature and timing). [P]		
J. Outreach		
1. Identify target groups, their information sources, and locations. [P]		
2. Develop program outreach plan and materials. [P]		
3. Orient and train outreach personnel as needed. [P]		
4. Conduct outreach activities and monitor results regularly. [P]		
5. Review and revise outreach plan and activities as needed. [P]		
K. Public Information and Public Relations		
1. Prepare and disseminate press release on grant award. [P]		
2. Identify and plan for other public information and public relations opportunities within program. [P]		
3. Implement plan (prepare press releases and press kits, gain coverage for events and photo opportunities, disseminate relevant publications and reports). [P]		
L. Program Monitoring and Control		
1. Program or unit head meets regularly with in-house supervisor to monitor progress against this program or unit work plan and specific program or unit goals. [P]		
2. Identify, plan, and take corrective action as needed. [P]		
3. Request any needed program or activity modifications in writing, including extension, if allowed and needed. [P]		
M. Budget Monitoring and Control		
1. Prepare internal operating program or unit budget.		
2. Disseminate operating budget as appropriate.		
3. Program or unit head communicates regularly with finance regarding expenses, budget, and finances. [P]		
4. Identify, plan, and take corrective action as required. [P]		
5. Request budget modifications in writing as needed. [P]		
6. Request carryover of funds, if allowed and needed. [P]		
N. Any Other Major Activities, Objectives, or Milestones		
1. Identify specific action steps for reaching each. [P]		
2. Create or modify relevant policies and procedures as needed for program or unit services and activities. [P]		

EXHIBIT A.1   **Blank Master for Creating a Program or Unit Work Plan** *(continued)*

PROJECT PHASES AND ACTION STEPS	RESPONSIBILITY	TARGET DATE
3. Identify and schedule access to needed outside services (for example, printing or consultants). [P]		
4. Create needed materials. [P]		
O. Program and Financial Evaluation		
1. Begin evaluation data collection and analysis. [P]		
2. Prepare and submit required in-house evaluations.		
3. Prepare and submit interim and final funding source evaluations as required (specify evaluation nature and timing). [P]		
P. For Continuation		
1. Identify in-house person to maintain ongoing liaison with funding source higher-ups.		
2. Identify in-house person to maintain liaison with funding source program representative.		
3. Plan for site visits by representative of current funding source.		
4. Prepare and submit all in-house and funding source program reports on time.		
5. Prepare and submit all in-house and funding source financial reports on time.		
6. Regularly gather and analyze evaluation data.		
7. Prepare and submit all evaluation reports as required.		
8. Identify potential funding sources for program refunding and continuation or expansion.		
9. Prepare and submit proposals for program refunding and continuation or expansion.		
10. Negotiate with potential refunding sources as needed. [P]		

RESOURCE B

Sample Blank Budget Formats

Contents

EXHIBIT B.1   **Blank Community Services Organization Budget Format**

REVENUE   AMOUNTS

Revenue Sources

_____   _____

_____   _____

_____   _____

Total Revenue   _____

EXPENDITURES

Categories

Salaries   _____

Employee Benefits   _____

Payroll Taxes   _____

Nonpayroll Insurance   _____

Professional Fees   _____

Supplies   _____

Telephone   _____

Postage   _____

Rent and Mortgage   _____

Utilities   _____

Building and Grounds Maintenance   _____

Rental and Maintenance of Equipment   _____

Purchase of Equipment   _____

Printing and Publications   _____

Travel   _____

Conferences, Conventions, and Meetings   _____

Membership Dues   _____

Awards and Grants   _____

Miscellaneous   _____

Capital   _____

Total Expenditures   _____

REVENUE OVER/(UNDER) EXPENSES   _____

EXHIBIT B.2   **Blank Expense Budget Format for a Museum Curatorial Department**

EXPENSE CATEGORIES	AMOUNT
Salaries (Full Time)	_____
Salaries (Part Time and Interns)	_____
Consultant Services	_____
Benefits (Allocated)	_____
Office Supplies	_____
Printing	_____
Photography/Microfilm	_____
Binding Supplies and Services	_____
Conservation Supplies and Services	_____
Postage and Messenger Service	_____
Freight	_____
Dues, Subscriptions, and Publications	_____
Travel (Local)	_____
Travel (Conferences)	_____
Registration Fees and Meetings	_____
Travel (Research)	_____
Entertainment	_____
Photocopy Expense	_____
Telephone	_____
Equipment	_____
Furniture and Fixtures	_____
Miscellaneous	_____
TOTAL CURATORIAL DEPARTMENT EXPENDITURES	_____

EXHIBIT B.3   **Blank Expense Budget Format for a Building and Security Department**

EXPENSE CATEGORIES	AMOUNT
Salaries (Full Time)	_____
Salaries (Part Time and Interns)	_____
Consultant Services	_____
Benefits (Allocated)	_____
Office Supplies	_____
Printing	_____
Photography/Microfilm	_____
Postage and Messenger Service	_____
Freight	_____
Dues, Subscriptions, and Publications	_____
Travel (Local)	_____
Travel (Conferences)	_____
Registration Fees and Meetings	_____
Entertainment	_____
Flowers	_____
Building and Space Maintenance	_____
Housekeeping Supplies	_____
Food and Beverage Supplies	_____
Photocopying Expense	_____
Telephone	_____
Utilities	_____
Equipment	_____
Furniture and Fixtures	_____
Gardening	_____
Construction	_____
Renovation	_____
Other Professional Fees	_____
Advertising	_____
TOTAL BUILDING AND SECURITY DEPARTMENT EXPENSES	_____

EXHIBIT B.4   Blank Expense Budget Format for a Membership Department

EXPENSE CATEGORIES	AMOUNT
Salaries (Full Time)	_____
Salaries (Part Time and Interns)	_____
Consultant Services	_____
Benefits (Allocated)	_____
Office Supplies	_____
Printing	_____
Photography/Microfilm	_____
Postage and Messenger Service	_____
Freight	_____
Dues, Subscriptions, and Publications	_____
Travel (Local)	_____
Travel (Conferences)	_____
Registration Fees and Meetings	_____
Entertainment	_____
Flowers	_____
Bank Fees and Credit Card Expenses	_____
Photocopy Expense	_____
Telephone	_____
Equipment	_____
Furniture and Fixtures	_____
Computer and Software Maintenance	_____
Advertising and Public Relations	_____
TOTAL MEMBERSHIP DEPARTMENT EXPENSES	======

EXHIBIT B.5	Blank Budget Form (with Instructions)

(If the funding source does not provide a budget format, you may cross out and add to the following categories and subcategories to arrive at a desired budget format.)

I. Personnel Costs

A. Employee Salaries

(Include number and title of position, percentage of time working [100 percent is full time] and annual salary.)

Administrative and Fiscal/Bookkeeping Staff

Supervisory Staff

Direct Service Staff

Secretarial and Clerical Staff

Other Staff (if applicable)

Subtotal, Employee Salaries $ _____

B. Employee Fringe Benefits

(Include FICA, SUI, workers' compensation, and any other fringe benefits, such as health insurance and pension.)

For All Full-Time Employees

For All Part-Time Employees

Subtotal, Employee Fringe Benefits $ _____

C. Consultants and Contract Services

(List by functions or areas of expertise, such as medical, educational, psychiatric, psychological, legal, accounting, data processing, payroll preparation, and management services; number of hours or days of service needed; hourly or daily rate for each; and total amount for each.)

Subtotal, Consultants and Contract Services $ _____

TOTAL, PERSONNEL COSTS $ _____

II. Other Than Personnel Costs

A. Materials and Supplies

(List items and amounts under each budget category.)

Consumable Medical Supplies

Consumable Program Supplies

Consumable Vocational Supplies

Consumable Recreational Supplies

Consumable Laundry Supplies

Consumable Housekeeping Supplies

Consumable Office Supplies

Food and Beverages (including number and cost of snacks and meals to be served to clients and staff)

Subtotal, Materials and Supplies $ _____

EXHIBIT B.5   **Blank Budget Form (with Instructions)** *(continued)*

B. Facilities

(Describe facilities and costs, including number, square footage, annual rent, and cost of maintenance and repairs of facilities needed to implement the program.)

Facilities for Program Administration

Facilities for Program Services and Activities

Facilities for Client Residences

Facilities for Staff Offices

Any Other Facilities Needed

Subtotal, Facilities $ _____

C. Insurance Needed for Program Facilities

(Identify insurance needed for each facility or all of them; include amounts of coverage and annual premiums.)

Subtotal, Facilities Insurance $ _____

D. Specific Assistance to Be Provided to Clients

(Describe the following amounts per client per month and the total for all clients for the year.)

Allowances (Cash Payments) to Clients

Personal Items (Such as Health and Beauty Aids for Hygiene, Clothing, Personal Appearance)

Any Other Specific Assistance to Clients

Subtotal, Assistance to Clients $ _____

E. Travel and Transportation for Program Operations

Costs of Transporting Clients (include nature, purpose, estimated mileage)

Costs of Staff Travel (include nature, purpose, estimated mileage)

Costs of Vehicles to Be Operated (include type, number, and uses)

Costs of Vehicle and/or Travel-Related Insurance (include type and amount of coverage)

Subtotal, Travel and Transportation $ _____

F. Training, Conferences, and Meetings

Training for Staff and/or Clients (include nature, purpose, hours/days, numbers of trainees)

Staff Attendance at Meetings and Conferences (include nature, purpose, location, duration)

Subtotal, Training, Conferences, and Meetings $ _____

EXHIBIT B.5   Blank Budget Form (with Instructions) *(continued)*

G. **Membership Dues for Business, Professional, or Technical Organizations**

(Include organization names, number of memberships, and amounts of dues.)

Subtotal, Membership Dues $ _____

H. **Subscriptions to Professional Publications**

(Include names or type and number of professional publications and annual subscription rates.)

Subtotal, Subscriptions $ _____

I. **Other Insurance Needed for the Program**

(Include the kind of insurance and amount of coverage.)

Subtotal, Other Insurance $ _____

J. **Miscellaneous Goods and Services Not Identified Earlier**

(Include the kinds of goods or services and their purpose or intended use in the program.)

Subtotal, Miscellaneous $ _____

TOTAL, OTHER THAN PERSONNEL COSTS $ _____

GRAND TOTAL, ALL PROGRAM COSTS $ _____

EXHIBIT B.6   **Blank Budget Format for a Museum Exhibition**

Exhibition Title: _____ Current Date: _____

EXHIBITION EXPENSES	AMOUNT
Assembly and Dispersal	_____
Insurance	_____
Installation	_____
Materials	_____
Signage	_____
Wall texts	_____
Conservation	_____
Educational Programs	_____
Visitors' information sheet	_____
Lectures	_____
Concerts	_____
Audiovisual production	_____
Gallery talks	_____
Special Fundraising Events	_____
Opening for sponsors	_____
Opening for supporters	_____
Dinner	_____
Publicity and Advertising	_____
Paid advertising	_____
Photography	_____
Press kits	_____
Banners	_____
Brochure	_____
Outdoor signage	_____
Posters	_____
Catalogue	_____
Author's fee and expenses	_____
Printing/Design	_____
Per Diem and Travel to Openings	_____
Honorarium for Lecturers	_____
Contingency	_____
Total Exhibition Expenses	_____

EXHIBIT B.6 **Blank Budget Format for a Museum Exhibition** *(continued)*

EXHIBITION INCOME	AMOUNT
Grants	_____
Admission Fees	_____
Catalogue Sales	_____
Poster Sales	_____
Donations	_____
Special Fundraising Events	_____
Fellows' opening	_____
Friends' opening	_____
Dinner	_____
Educational Program Fees	_____
Lectures (three)	_____
Concerts	_____
Rental of audiocassettes	_____
Sale of videotapes	_____
Gallery talks	_____
Total Exhibition Income	_____
EXHIBITION SURPLUS/(DEFICIT)	_____

EXHIBIT B.7   **Sample Capital Project Budget**

	TOTAL ANNUAL COSTS		
CAPITAL PROJECTS:	FY 1998	FY 1999	FY 2000
Safety and Environmental Compliance			
Strategic Initiatives			
Minor Equipment (less than $500/unit)			
Major Equipment (more than $500/unit)			
Major Construction			
Miscellaneous Improvements			
Contingency			
TOTALS			

EXHIBIT B.8   **Sample Capital Budget for a Building**

PROJECT COMPONENTS:	TOTAL BUDGET	EXPENDITURES TO DATE	FY 1998 BUDGET
Architectural and Engineering Design			
Building Construction			
Tenant Improvement Allowance			
Heating and Cooling Systems			
Property Management and Lease Negotiations			
Telephone Data System			
Contingency			
TOTALS			

Examples of Financial Reports for Analyzing and Monitoring Income and Expenses

Following are examples of financial report formats for analyzing and monitoring budgeted versus actual income and expense figures. Some are completed examples; others are left blank. You will notice a variety of different styles, degrees of detail, and emphasis in the following sample reports, which illustrate the many options for analyzing and monitoring budgeted versus actual expenses.

Contents

EXHIBIT C.1 **Sample Three-Month Line-Item Financial Report**

ABC Nonprofit
Line-Item Report
for the Three Months Ended March 31, 1998[a]

	APPROVED ANNUAL BUDGET	CURRENT MONTH ACTUAL	YEAR-TO-DATE ACTUAL
Support and revenue:			
Grants	$43,000	$1,000	$7,500
Government funds	0	0	0
United Way	23,000	3,000	5,000
Fees	2,000	100	500
Corporate gifts	11,500	850	5,000
Other	8,650	500	4,500
Total support and revenue:	88,150	5,450	22,500
Expenses:			
Salaries and benefits:			
Permanent staff	67,080	2,785	6,406
Temporary staff	4,000	626	1,440
Operating expenses:			
Office supplies	2,000	112	258
Telephone	1,800	78	179
Rent	2,400	200	460
Utilities	1,800	461	1,060
Insurance	2,000	104	239
Printing	1,700	92	212
Postage	1,350	51	117
Equipment rental	900	76	175
Equipment/fixed assets:			
Office furniture	300	200	460
Computer equipment	1,500	0	0
Other:			
Memberships	120	10	23
Staff training	0	0	0
Consultant fees	700	211	485
Publications	0	0	0
Total expenses:	87,650	5,006	11,514
Excess (deficiency) of support over (under) expenses:	$500	$444	$10,986

[a]Fiscal year is calendar year.

EXHIBIT C.2   **Sample Monthly Financial Report**

ABC Nonprofit
Monthly Report
for the One Month and Three Months Ended March 31, 1998

	Prior Year Actual	Approved Annual Budget	Revised Annual Budget	Current Month Actual	Year-to-Date Actual
Support and revenue:					
Grants	$50,000	$50,000	$50,000	$10,000	$30,000
Membership dues	50,000	55,000	100,000	10,000	30,000
Corporate gifts	100,000	110,000	115,000	25,000	50,000
United Way	65,000	70,000	50,000	10,000	30,000
Other	25,000	30,000	25,000	500	1,500
Total support and revenue:	290,000	315,000	340,000	55,500	141,500
Expenses:					
Salaries	140,000	156,000	250,000	21,000	63,000
Benefits	29,000	31,000	50,000	4,200	12,600
Temporary staff	5,000	4,500	5,000	297	891
Office supplies	7,500	7,000	3,000	112	336
Telephone	1,500	1,500	500	78	234
Utilities	2,500	2,600	4,500	661	1,983
Printing	5,600	4,000	450	92	276
Insurance	900	900	900	500	1,500
Postage	300	300	300	51	153
Equipment rental	400	500	500	76	228
Equipment purchase	900	500	1,000	0	0
Maintenance	12,000	10,000	500	70	210
Consultant fees	55,000	25,000	20,000	1,500	4,500
Total expenses:	260,600	243,800	336,650	28,637	85,911
Excess (deficiency) of support and revenue over (under) expenses:	$29,400	$71,200	$3,350	$26,863	$55,589

EXHIBIT C.3   Sample Quarterly Financial Report

ABC Nonprofit
Quarterly Report
for the Period January 1, 1998, to March 31, 1998[a]

	CURRENT QUARTER BUDGET	CURRENT QUARTER ACTUAL	AMOUNT OF VARIANCE	PERCENTAGE OF VARIANCE	YEAR TO DATE	APPROVED BUDGET
Support and revenue:						
Grants	$50,000	$50,000	$0	0	50,000	$50,000
Membership dues	2,000	1,500	−500	−25	10,000	55,000
Corporate gifts	30,000	27,000	−3,000	−10	90,000	110,000
United Way	70,000	70,000	0	0	70,000	70,000
Other	5,000	2,000	−3,000	−60	20,000	30,000
Total support and revenue:	157,000	150,500	−6,500	−4	240,000	315,000
Expenses:						
Personnel:						
Salaried staff	30,000	30,000	0	0	130,000	156,000
Hourly staff	0	0	0		4,500	4,500
Benefits	6,000	6,000	0	0	16,000	31,000
Materials and supplies:					0	0
Office supplies	1,000	1,000	0	0	5,000	7,000
Postage	500	450	50	10	450	1,300
Printing	2,500	2,700	−200	−8	2,700	4,000
Insurance	500	400	100	20	400	900
Telephone	300	250	50	17	1,250	1,500
Utilities	200	200	0	0	1,200	2,600
Consultants	0	0	0	0	15,000	25,000
Maintenance	400	400	0	0	8,100	10,000
Equipment rental	2,500	1,500	1,000	40	5,500	7,500
Other	5,000	2,500	2,500	50	5,500	7,500
Total expenses:	48,900	45,400	3,500	7	195,600	258,800
Excess (deficiency) of support and revenue over (under) expenses:	$108,100	$105,100	($3,000)	−3	$44,400	$56,200

[a]Fiscal year ends June 30.

EXHIBIT C.4 **Sample Budget Variance Report**

ABC Nonprofit
Budget Variance Report
for the Ten Months Ended October 31, 1998

	ANNUAL BUDGET	YEAR-TO-DATE BUDGET	YEAR-TO-DATE ACTUAL	YEAR-TO-DATE PERCENTAGE VARIANCE	YEAR-TO-DATE $ VARIANCE
Revenue:					
Grants	$320,000	$266,667	$220,000	−18	−$46,667
Fundraising	150,000	125,000	75,000	−40	−50,000
Dues and fees	70,000	58,333	54,000	−7	−4,333
Total	$540,000	$450,000	$349,000	−22	−$101,000
Expenses:					
Personnel	$360,000	$300,000	$275,000	8	$25,000
Supplies	50,000	41,667	45,000	−8	−3,333
Services	30,000	25,000	25,000	0	0
Equipment	100,000	83,333	90,000	−8	−6,667
Total	$540,000	$450,000	$435,000	3	$15,000

EXHIBIT C.5 Sample Management Report—Income and Expenses

ABC Nonprofit

Sample Management Report for Monitoring Income and Expenses for the Nine Months Ending September 30, 1998

	Annual Budget	Year to Date	Difference	Prorated Budget	Year to Date	Difference	Monthly Budget	Month to Date	Monthly Difference
Support and revenue:									
Contributions	$196,851	$124,403	−$72,448	$147,638	$124,403	−$23,235	$16,404	$3,450	−$12,954
Membership dues	14,000	12,355	−1,645	10,500	12,355	1,855	1,167	1,150	−17
Conferences and seminars	2,000	8,327	6,327	1,500	8,327	6,827	167	18	−149
Interest	4,000	3,160	−840	3,000	3,160	160	333	250	−83
Total support and revenue:	216,851	148,245	−68,606	162,638	148,245	−14,393	18,071	4,868	−13,203
Expenses:									
Salaries	115,000	73,250	41,750	86,250	73,250	13,000	9,583	7,812	1,771
Fringe	23,000	8,288	14,712	17,250	8,288	8,962	1,917	655	1,262
Professional	13,000	4,693	8,307	9,750	4,693	5,057	1,083	864	219
Travel	3,000	2,279	721	2,250	2,279	−29	250	94	156
Seminars	4,000	3,254	746	3,000	3,254	−254	333	508	−175
Office	14,500	7,919	6,581	10,875	7,919	2,956	1,208	612	596
Utilities and telephone	8,000	4,730	3,270	6,000	4,730	1,270	667	510	157
Supplies and postage	8,500	4,983	3,517	6,375	4,983	1,392	708	619	89
Insurance	1,000	831	169	750	831	−81	83	585	−502
Printing	5,000	6,683	−1,683	3,750	6,683	−2,933	417	866	−449
Subscriptions	2,000	530	1,470	1,500	530	970	167	0	167
Training	2,000	368	1,632	1,500	368	1,132	167	0	167
Refunds	0	85	−85	0	85	−85	0	85	−85
Miscellaneous/contingency	1,000	562	438	750	562	188	83	20	63
Total expenses	200,000	118,455	81,545	150,000	118,455	31,545	16,666	13,230	3,436
Excess (deficiency) of support and revenue over (under) expenses:	$16,851	$29,790	$12,939	$12,638	$29,790	$17,152	$1,405	−$8,362	−$9,767

ABC Nonprofit
Management Report for Administration
for the Period January 1, 1998, to April 30, 1998

EXPENSES	ANNUAL BUDGET 1/1/98–12/31/98	ACTUAL 1/1/98–4/30/98	BALANCE REMAINING	PRORATED BUDGET 1/1/98–4/30/98	ACTUAL 1/1/98–4/30/98	$ VARIANCE	PERCENTAGE VARIANCE	BUDGET MONTH OF 4/98	EXPENSES MONTH OF 4/98	MONTHLY $ VARIANCE	MONTHLY PERCENTAGE VARIANCE
Personnel	210,000	68,789	141,211	70,000	68,789	1,211	2	17,500	17,241	259	1
Fringe benefits	48,000	15,921	32,079	16,000	15,921	79	0	4,000	3,987	13	0
Consultants	12,000	4,200	7,800	4,000	4,200	-200	-5	1,000	950	50	5
Travel	6,000	2,850	3,150	2,000	2,850	-850	-43	500	1,350	-850	-170
Rent	36,000	11,637	24,363	12,000	11,637	363	3	3,000	2,705	295	10
Supplies	9,000	4,839	4,161	3,000	4,839	-1,839	-61	750	2,109	-1,359	-181
Rent, purchase,	12,000	1,385	10,615	4,000	1,385	2,615	65	1,000	345	655	66
Other	18,000	5,878	12,122	6,000	5,878	122	2	1,500	1,311	189	13
TOTAL	$351,000	$115,499	$235,501	$117,000	$115,499	$1,501	1	$29,250	$29,998	-$748	-3

EXHIBIT C.7   Budgeted Versus Actual Year-to-Date Income and Expenses for a Small Foundation (by Unrestricted and Restricted Funds)

	UNRESTRICTED FUNDS		RESTRICTED FUNDS	
	ANNUAL BUDGET	ACTUAL	ANNUAL BUDGET	ACTUAL
INCOME:				
Contributions	_____	_____	_____	_____
Royalties	_____	_____	_____	_____
Conference Registration Fees	_____	_____	_____	_____
Publications	_____	_____	_____	_____
Interest and Other Income	_____	_____	_____	_____
Transfer from ABC Foundation	_____	_____	_____	_____
Total Income	_____	_____	_____	_____
PROGRAM EXPENSES:				
Conference	_____	_____	_____	_____
Publications	_____	_____	_____	_____
Awards	_____	_____	_____	_____
Fund Development	_____	_____	_____	_____
General and Administrative Expenses	_____	_____	_____	_____
Internship Program	_____	_____	_____	_____
Grants	_____	_____	_____	_____
Total Program Expenses	_____	_____	_____	_____
EXCESS REVENUE OVER EXPENSE BEFORE DEPRECIATION	_____	_____	_____	_____

EXHIBIT C.8

**Budgeted Versus Actual Year-to-Date Income and
Expenses for a Small Foundation (by Major Activities)**

	CONFERENCES		PUBLICATIONS		AWARDS AND PROGRAMS		ADMINISTRATION		FUND DEVELOPMENT	
	ANNUAL BUDGET	YEAR-TO-DATE ACTUAL	ANNUAL BUDGET	YEAR-TO-DATE ACTUAL	ANNUAL BUDGET	YEAR-TO-DATE ACTUAL	ANNUAL BUDGET	YEAR-TO-DATE ACTUAL	ANNUAL BUDGET	YEAR-TO-DATE ACTUAL
INCOME:										
Contributions	___	___	___	___	___	___	___	___	___	___
Conference Registration Fees	___	___	___	___	___	___	___	___	___	___
Interest and Other Income	___	___	___	___	___	___	___	___	___	___
Royalties from Publications	___	___	___	___	___	___	___	___	___	___
Total Income	___	___	___	___	___	___	___	___	___	___
PROGRAM EXPENSES:										
Salaries and Payroll Taxes	___	___	___	___	___	___	___	___	___	___
Fringe Benefits at 24 Percent	___	___	___	___	___	___	___	___	___	___
Total Salaries and Benefits	___	___	___	___	___	___	___	___	___	___
Professional Fees	___	___	___	___	___	___	___	___	___	___
Development Costs	___	___	___	___	___	___	___	___	___	___
Travel and Entertainment	___	___	___	___	___	___	___	___	___	___

EXHIBIT C.8 Budgeted Versus Actual Year-to-Date Income and Expenses for a Small Foundation (by Major Activities) *(continued)*

	CONFERENCES		PUBLICATIONS		AWARDS AND PROGRAMS		ADMINISTRATION		FUND DEVELOPMENT	
	ANNUAL BUDGET	YEAR-TO-DATE ACTUAL	ANNUAL BUDGET	YEAR-TO-DATE ACTUAL	ANNUAL BUDGET	YEAR-TO-DATE ACTUAL	ANNUAL BUDGET	YEAR-TO-DATE ACTUAL	ANNUAL BUDGET	YEAR-TO-DATE ACTUAL
Membership and Dues										
Books and Subscriptions										
Printing and Mailings										
Office Expenses										
Conference										
Meeting Expenses										
Miscellaneous Expenses										
Total Expenses										
EXCESS REVENUE OVER EXPENSES:										

	CURRENT MONTH			YEAR TO DATE		
	MANAGEMENT COMPANY 1	MANAGEMENT COMPANY 2	TOTAL	MANAGEMENT COMPANY 1	MANAGEMENT COMPANY 2	TOTAL
REVENUE:						
Rental Income	——	——	——	——	——	——
Management Fees	——	——	——	——	——	——
Interest Income	——	——	——	——	——	——
Other Investment Income	——	——	——	——	——	——
Social Service Income	——	——	——	——	——	——
Other Revenue	——	——	——	——	——	——
Total Revenue	——	——	——	——	——	——
EXPENSES:						
Personnel Salaries	——	——	——	——	——	——
Fringe Benefits	——	——	——	——	——	——
Administrative Expenses	——	——	——	——	——	——
Utilities	——	——	——	——	——	——
Operating and Maintenance	——	——	——	——	——	——
Taxes and Insurance	——	——	——	——	——	——
Other Expenses	——	——	——	——	——	——
Total Expenses	——	——	——	——	——	——
EXCESS OF REVENUE OVER EXPENSES:	——	——	——	——	——	——

	BUDGETED			ACTUAL		DIFFERENCE
	ANNUAL	YEAR TO DATE	CURRENT MONTH	YEAR TO DATE	CURRENT MONTH	YEAR-TO-DATE BUDGET VERSUS ACTUAL
REVENUE:						
Rental Income						
Management Fees						
Interest and Investment Income						
Social Service Income						
Other Revenue						
Total Revenue						
EXPENSES:						
Personnel Salaries						
Fringe Benefits						
Administrative Expenses						
Utilities						
Operating and Maintenance						
Taxes and Insurance						
Other Expenses						
Total Expenses						
EXCESS OF REVENUE OVER EXPENSES:						

EXHIBIT **A Housing Development Corporation's Departmental**
C.11 **Revenue and Expense Report Format**

	GENERAL FUNDS	PROGRAM A	PROGRAM B	PROGRAM C	PROGRAM D	TOTAL
REVENUE:						
Corporation and Foundation Grants	_____	_____	_____	_____	_____	_____
Governmental Grants	_____	_____	_____	_____	_____	_____
Marketing Fees	_____	_____	_____	_____	_____	_____
Development Fees	_____	_____	_____	_____	_____	_____
Partnership Management Fees	_____	_____	_____	_____	_____	_____
Rental Income	_____	_____	_____	_____	_____	_____
Management Fees	_____	_____	_____	_____	_____	_____
Interest/Investment Income	_____	_____	_____	_____	_____	_____
Fundraising	_____	_____	_____	_____	_____	_____
Social Service Income	_____	_____	_____	_____	_____	_____
Other Revenue	_____	_____	_____	_____	_____	_____
Total Revenue	_____	_____	_____	_____	_____	_____
EXPENSES:						
Personnel Salaries	_____	_____	_____	_____	_____	_____
Fringe Benefits	_____	_____	_____	_____	_____	_____
Administrative Expenses	_____	_____	_____	_____	_____	_____
Utilities	_____	_____	_____	_____	_____	_____
Operating and Maintenance	_____	_____	_____	_____	_____	_____
Taxes and Insurance	_____	_____	_____	_____	_____	_____
Other	_____	_____	_____	_____	_____	_____
Total Expenses	_____	_____	_____	_____	_____	_____

EXHIBIT C.11

A Housing Development Corporation's Departmental Revenue and Expense Report Format *(continued)*

	GENERAL FUNDS	PROGRAM A	PROGRAM B	PROGRAM C	PROGRAM D	TOTAL
OTHER ITEMS:						
Debt Service	___	___	___	___	___	___
Capital Expenditures	___	___	___	___	___	___
Total Other Items	___	___	___	___	___	___
TOTAL EXPENSES AND OTHER ITEMS:	___	___	___	___	___	___
EXCESS OF REVENUE OVER EXPENSES:						

Tools for Analyzing Financial Reports and Planning Corrective Action

RESOURCE
D

Contents

A. Tips for Analyzing Financial Reports and Planning Corrective Action

There are two basic ways to analyze most financial reports:

1. *Actual versus budgeted.* Compare the actual figures reported for the current period (month, quarter, or year to date) to the figures budgeted for the same period.

2. *Same time this year and last year.* Compare the actual figures reported for the current period to the actual figures reported for the same period a year earlier.

Use both methods. Then take what you have learned from the comparisons to identify problem areas, set goals, and assign responsibilities and deadlines for carrying out corrective action.

Do not forget to update cash flow projections at least a month in advance. A budget report that indicates a surplus or deficit does not tell you anything about how much cash is actually available for paying bills. You need to monitor cash flow separately, as detailed in Chapters Two, Eight, and Twenty.

B. Authors' Note

The following material should be modified to reflect the degree of detail your organization requires for specific budgeting processes and submissions. For example, some of the formats and information may be too detailed for board-level review, such as Section VI of Exhibit D.1—Analyzing Bad Debts. However, much of the information in other areas, such as those detailing income and expenses, will be appropriately detailed for submission to the board, management, and financial staff. Regardless of how you use these tools, we advise that organizations examine and complete all material sections before starting next year's budget.

EXHIBIT **Worksheet for Analyzing Financial Reports**
D.1 **and Planning Corrective Action**

I. Get copies of the same financial report for each of the periods you want to compare.

II. Compare totals for the current and prior periods.

   A. Look for any changes in totals.

   1. Did total income: ☐ Increase? ☐ Decrease? ☐ Stay about the same?
      a. The actual change: ☐ Plus $ _____ or ____ percent ☐ Minus $ _____ or ____ percent
   2. Did total expenses: ☐ Increase? ☐ Decrease? ☐ Stay about the same?
      a. The actual change: ☐ Plus $ _____ or ____ percent ☐ Minus $ _____ or ____ percent

III. Identify current and prior surpluses or deficits.

   A. Compare total income to total expenses.

   1. There seems to be a current: ☐ Surplus of $ _____. ☐ Deficit of $ _____.
   2. The prior period shows a: ☐ Surplus of $ _____. ☐ Deficit of $ _____.

IV. Analyze current and prior income.

   A. Did the ratio of total income coming from specific sources change significantly between the prior and current periods? ☐ Yes. ☐ No.

   1. If yes, which ratio(s) changed?
      a. The ratio of _____ to _____ changed from ___ : ___ to ___ : ___.
      b. The ratio of _____ to _____ changed from ___ : ___ to ___ : ___.
      c. The ratio of _____ to _____ changed from ___ : ___ to ___ : ___.

   B. Look for any changes in individual sources of income:

   1. Which income from which source(s) went up and by how much?
      a. Income from _____ went up by $ _____ or ___ percent.
      b. Income from _____ went up by $ _____ or ___ percent.
      c. Income from _____ went up by $ _____ or ___ percent.
      d. Income from _____ went up by $ _____ or ___ percent.

   2. Which income from which source(s) went down and by how much?
      a. Income from _____ went down by $ _____ or ___ percent.
      b. Income from _____ went down by $ _____ or ___ percent.
      c. Income from _____ went down by $ _____ or ___ percent.
      d. Income from _____ went down by $ _____ or ___ percent.

   3. Which income from which source(s) stayed about the same?
      a. Income from _____ stayed about the same.
      b. Income from _____ stayed about the same.
      c. Income from _____ stayed about the same.
      d. Income from _____ stayed about the same.

EXHIBIT D.1   **Worksheet for Analyzing Financial Reports and Planning Corrective Action** *(continued)*

C. **Specific factors or circumstances that may have helped make income go up:**

1. Income Source: _____ went up because _____

_____

2. Income Source: _____ went up because _____

_____

3. Income Source: _____ went up because _____

_____

4. Income Source: _____ went up because _____

_____

D. **Specific factors or circumstances that may have helped make income go down:**

1. Income Source: _____ went down because: _____

_____

2. Income Source: _____ went down because: _____

_____

3. Income Source: _____ went down because: _____

_____

4. Income Source: _____ went down because: _____

_____

E. **Specific factors or circumstances that may have helped keep income about the same:**

1. Income Source: _____ stayed about the same because: _____

_____

2. Income Source: _____ stayed about the same because: _____

_____

3. Income Source: _____ stayed about the same because: _____

_____

F. **Analyze the specific factors or circumstances you identified:**

1. If the specific factors or circumstances you identified had been known as soon as they occurred, which ones could someone in your organization have done something about?

FACTOR/CIRCUMSTANCE	WHAT COULD HAVE BEEN DONE ABOUT IT?	BY WHOM?
a. _____	_____	_____
b. _____	_____	_____
c. _____	_____	_____
d. _____	_____	_____
e. _____	_____	_____
f. _____	_____	_____
g. _____	_____	_____
h. _____	_____	_____
i. _____	_____	_____
j. _____	_____	_____
k. _____	_____	_____
l. _____	_____	_____
m. _____	_____	_____

EXHIBIT **Worksheet for Analyzing Financial Reports**
D.1 **and Planning Corrective Action** *(continued)*

2. If the specific factors/circumstances you identified had been known as soon as they occurred, which ones could someone in your organization have done nothing about?

FACTOR/CIRCUMSTANCE   WHY COULD NOTHING BE DONE ABOUT IT?

a. _____   _____

b. _____   _____

c. _____   _____

d. _____   _____

e. _____   _____

f. _____   _____

g. _____   _____

h. _____   _____

i.   _____

j. _____   _____

k. _____   _____

l. _____   _____

m. _____   _____

V. Analyze current and prior expenses.

A. Did the ratios of major expense categories change significantly when compared to each other?   ☐ Yes.   ☐ No.

1. If yes, which ratio(s) changed?

a. The ratio of _____ to _____ changed from ___ : ___ to ___ : ___.

b. The ratio of _____ to _____ changed from ___ : ___ to ___ : ___.

c. The ratio of _____ to _____ changed from ___ : ___ to ___ : ___.

d. The ratio of _____ to _____ changed from ___ : ___ to ___ : ___.

e. The ratio of _____ to _____ changed from ___ : ___ to ___ : ___.

B. Look for any changes in individual expense categories.

1. Which expense categories went up significantly and by how much?

a. Expenses for _____ went up by $ _____ or ____ percent.

b. Expenses for _____ went up by $ _____ or ____ percent.

c. Expenses for _____ went up by $ _____ or ____ percent.

d. Expenses for _____ went up by $ _____ or ____ percent.

e. Expenses for _____ went up by $ _____ or ____ percent.

f. Expenses for _____ went up by $ _____ or ____ percent.

g. Expenses for _____ went up by $ _____ or ____ percent.

2. Which expense categories went down significantly and by how much?

a. Expenses for _____ went down by $ _____ or ____ percent.

b. Expenses for _____ went down by $ _____ or ____ percent.

c. Expenses for _____ went down by $ _____ or ____ percent.

d. Expenses for _____ went down by $ _____ or ____ percent.

e. Expenses for _____ went down by $ _____ or ____ percent.

f. Expenses for _____ went down by $ _____ or ____ percent.

g. Expenses for _____ went down by $ _____ or ____ percent.

EXHIBIT D.1 **Worksheet for Analyzing Financial Reports and Planning Corrective Action** *(continued)*

   3. Which expenses categories stayed about the same:

      a. Income from _____ stayed about the same.

      b. Income from _____ stayed about the same.

      c. Income from _____ stayed about the same.

      d. Income from _____ stayed about the same.

C. Specific factors or circumstances that may have helped make expenses go up:

   1. Expense category _____ went up $ _____ or ____ percent because: _____
_____

   2. Expense category _____ went up $ _____ or ____ percent because: _____
_____

   3. Expense category _____ went up $ _____ or ____ percent because: _____
_____

   4. Expense category _____ went up $ _____ or ____ percent because: _____
_____

   5. Expense category _____ went up $ _____ or ____ percent because: _____
_____

   6. Expense category _____ went up $ _____ or ____ percent because: _____
_____

   7. Expense category _____ went up $ _____ or ____ percent because: _____
_____

D. Specific factors or circumstances that may have helped make expenses go down:

   1. Expense category _____ went down $ _____ or ____ percent because: _____
_____

   2. Expense category _____ went down $ _____ or ____ percent because: _____
_____

   3. Expense category _____ went down $ _____ or ____ percent because: _____
_____

E. Specific factors or circumstances that may have helped keep expenses about the same:

   1. Expense category _____ stayed about the same because: _____
_____

   2. Expense category _____ stayed about the same because: _____
_____

   3. Expense category _____ stayed about the same because: _____
_____

   4. Expense category _____ stayed about the same because: _____
_____

EXHIBIT D.1   **Worksheet for Analyzing Financial Reports and Planning Corrective Action** *(continued)*

F. **Analyze the specific factors or circumstances that helped increase expenses:**

1. If the specific factors or circumstances you identified were recognized when they occurred, which ones could someone in the organization have done something about?

FACTOR/CIRCUMSTANCE	WHAT COULD HAVE BEEN DONE ABOUT IT?	BY WHOM?
a. _____	_____	_____
b. _____	_____	_____
c. _____	_____	_____
d. _____	_____	_____
e. _____	_____	_____
f. _____	_____	_____
g. _____	_____	_____
h. _____	_____	_____
i. _____	_____	_____
j. _____	_____	_____
k. _____	_____	_____
l. _____	_____	_____
m. _____	_____	_____

2. If the specific factors or circumstances you identified were recognized when they occurred, which ones could someone in your organization have done nothing about?

FACTOR/CIRCUMSTANCE	WHY COULD NOTHING BE DONE ABOUT IT?
a. _____	_____
b. _____	_____
c. _____	_____
d. _____	_____
e. _____	_____
f. _____	_____
g. _____	_____
h. _____	_____
i. _____	_____
j. _____	_____
k. _____	_____
l. _____	_____
m. _____	_____

VI. **Analyze bad debts.**

A. **What is the ratio of bad debts to income?**

1. Total bad debt is $ _____. Total income is $ _____. The ratio is ___ : ___.
2. Is this ratio too high, or is it acceptable? ☐ Acceptable. ☐ Too high.
3. How do you know? _____
_____.

**EXHIBIT
D.1**   **Worksheet for Analyzing Financial Reports
and Planning Corrective Action** *(continued)*

VII. Set goals for improvement.

A. What specific goals would you like to reach?

1. Income? _____
   _____
   _____.

2. Expenses? _____
   _____
   _____.

3. Bad debts? _____
   _____
   _____.

B. What specific things have to be done to reach each goal?

GOAL	ACTION(S) REQUIRED	BY WHOM AND WHEN?
1. _____ :	_____	_____
	_____	_____
	_____	_____
2. _____ :	_____	_____
	_____	_____
	_____	_____
3. _____ :	_____	_____
	_____	_____
	_____	_____
4. _____ :	_____	_____
	_____	_____
	_____	_____

C. Goals you plan to reach for any other specific items in this report:

REPORT ITEM	GOAL
1. _____ :	_____
2. _____ :	_____
3. _____ :	_____

D. What specific things have to be done to reach any additional goals?

GOAL	ACTION(S) REQUIRED	BY WHOM AND WHEN?
1. _____ :	_____	_____
	_____	_____
	_____	_____
2. _____ :	_____	_____
	_____	_____
	_____	_____
3. _____ :	_____	_____
	_____	_____
	_____	_____

EXHIBIT D.2 Sample Analysis of Individual Line-Item Expense Variances (Budgeted Versus Actual) in Excess of $3,000 or of 3 Percent

Program/Unit/Activity: _____ **Analysis Period:** _____

Note: Higher-than-budgeted expenses are in parentheses ["(82 percent)"], lower-than-expected expenses are not ["8 percent"].

Line Item	Year-to-Date Budget	Year-to-Date Actual	Dollar Variance	Percentage Variance	Variance Analysis
Salaries	$100,000	$92,000	$8,000	8 percent	To date 2 positions vacant; to be filled in June. No raises yet given; amount will depend in part on union negotiations. Union/nonunion raises expected to average about 4 percent in July.
Employee Benefits	10,000	9,100	900	9 percent	To date, 2 positions vacant; expected to be filled in June.
Payroll Taxes	10,000	8,700	1,300	13 percent	Variance causes same as for salaries.
Nonpayroll Insurance	5,000	9,100	(4,100)	(82 percent)	Large increase in malpractice insurance.
Professional Fees	4,000	640	3,360	84 percent	Expenditures uneven during the year.
Supplies	3,000	1,500	1,500	50 percent	Purchases uneven during the year.
Telephone	4,000	2,960	1,040	26 percent	Surplus due to staff vacancies.
Postage	1,000	550	450	45 percent	Expenditures below projected year to date.
Rent	30,000	30,000	0	0 percent	
Building and Grounds Maintenance	6,000	3,360	2,640	44 percent	Expenditures running below estimate (no snow to date).
Rent and Maintenance of Equipment	7,000	3,570	3,430	49 percent	Few repairs and rentals needed year to date.
Purchase of Equipment	2,000	0	2,000	100 percent	No equipment under $100 needed year to date.
Printing and Publications	2,000	1,520	480	24 percent	Expenditures uneven during year.
Travel	9,000	13,770	(4,770)	(53 percent)	Travel during summer will use surplus.
Conferences, Conventions, and Meetings	3,000	3,540	(540)	(18 percent)	An additional staff person sent to conference.
Membership Dues	1,000	1,540	(540)	(54 percent)	Dues paid primarily at start of year.
Awards and Grants	25,000	0	25,000	100 percent	No requests for grants to date.
Miscellaneous	5,000	2,450	2,550	51 percent	Expenditures uneven during year.
Fundraising	10,000	0	10,000	100 percent	Fundraising expenses for fall event.

Worksheet for Analyzing Line-Item Expense Variances (Budgeted Versus Actual)

BACKGROUND INFORMATION

1. Budget(s) Analyzed: _____.

2. Period Covered by Analysis: From _____ to _____.

3. Date Analysis Done: __/__/__.

4. Only Include Line-Item Variances in Excess of $_____ or of ____ Percent in This Analysis.

HOW TO USE THIS WORKSHEET

1. To analyze budgeted versus actual line-item variances, use photocopies of this worksheet.

2. Put higher-than-expected variances in parentheses ["(82 percent)"]; omit parentheses for lower-than-expected variances ["8 percent"].

FORM FOR ANALYZING BUDGETED VERSUS ACTUAL LINE-ITEM EXPENDITURE VARIANCES

LINE ITEM	YEAR-TO-DATE BUDGET	YEAR-TO-DATE ACTUAL	DOLLAR VARIANCE	PERCENTAGE VARIANCE	VARIANCE ANALYSIS
_____	_____	_____	_____	_____	_____
_____	_____	_____	_____	_____	_____
_____	_____	_____	_____	_____	_____
_____	_____	_____	_____	_____	_____
_____	_____	_____	_____	_____	_____
_____	_____	_____	_____	_____	_____
_____	_____	_____	_____	_____	_____

EXHIBIT D.4   Sample Analysis of Budgeted-Versus-Actual Expense Variances by Income Source

SOURCE OF INCOME	PERCENT OF YEAR ELAPSED	PERCENT FUNDS EXPENDED	EXPLANATION OF VARIANCE AND ACTION NEEDED
U.S. Department of Education	25	35	Services being provided faster than planned. *Monitor to avoid cost overrun.*
U.S. Department of Health and Human Services	25	10	Two vacant positions; personnel costs and services behind schedule. *Fill vacant positions.*
Community Development Block Grant	25	71	Overstaffed by 3; funds to be totally spent by June. *Transfer extra staff now.*
State Housing Authority	25	3	Number of tenants served is way behind plan. *Improve application processing.*
ABC Foundation	25	11	Services restricted to first-trimester pregnant women. *Speed up recruitment.*
DEF Foundation	25	0	Got funds 2 months late; staff being interviewed. *Get 3-month budget modification.*

EXHIBIT D.5   Blank Form for Analysis of Budgeted-Versus-Actual Expense Variances by Income Source

SOURCE OF INCOME	PERCENT OF YEAR ELAPSED	PERCENT FUNDS EXPENDED	EXPLANATION OF VARIANCE AND ACTION NEEDED
_____	_____	_____	_____
_____	_____	_____	_____
_____	_____	_____	_____
_____	_____	_____	_____
_____	_____	_____	_____
_____	_____	_____	_____

Example of a Detailed Organizationwide Expense Budget

Following is an organizationwide expense budget created for a nonprofit organization. The degree of detail represented would make this level of budget appropriate for presentation to most boards. Of course, depending on the organization, some boards require a more detailed budget, with all figures from program and unit budgets included. After the sample organizationwide expense budget, you will find a blank form for your use.

Contents

Exhibit E.1: Sample Detailed Organizationwide Expense Budget by Program

Exhibit E.2: Blank Detailed Organizationwide Expense Budget by Program

EXHIBIT E.1 Sample Detailed Organizationwide Expense Budget by Program

Budget Category	Total	Program 1	Program 2	Program 3	Program 4	Program 5	Program 6	Program 7
A. Personnel	$1,155,163	$523,281	$87,496	$4,426	$309,380	$86,858	$74,292	$67,430
B. Consultants and Professional Services	107,022	35,191	23,227	412	34,180	1,737	10,405	1,870
C. Materials and Supplies	114,613	43,608	9,922	2,879	36,129	15,169	2,708	4,198
D. Facility Costs	119,014	41,257	4,019	5,027	39,636	23,555	3,459	2,061
E. Specific Assistance to Clients	89,873	54,714	–	8,940	2,812	16,571	–	6,836
F. Other Costs	74,977	14,705	17,866	2,781	14,006	4,093	19,528	1,998
G. Total Operating Costs	1,658,662	712,756	142,530	24,465	436,143	147,983	110,392	84,393
H. Equipment (detail not shown)	69,189	69,189	–	–	–	–	–	–
I. Total Cost	$1,727,851	$781,945	$142,530	$24,465	$436,143	$147,983	$110,392	$84,393

Budget Category	Hours per Week	Total	Program 1	Program 2	Program 3	Program 4	Program 5	Program 6	Program 7
Personnel									
1. Chief Executive Officer	40	$59,676	$ —	$26,338	$ —	$15,009	$ —	$18,329	$ —
2. Bookkeeper	40	33,795	—	17,362	—	6,883	—	9,550	—
3. Admin. Assistant	40	—	—	—	—	—	—	—	—
4. Personnel Secretary	40	25,614	—	13,159	—	5,225	—	7,230	—
5. Acct. Secretary	40	17,458	—	8,994	—	3,585	—	4,879	—
6. Secretary	40	20,757	20,757	—	—	—	—	—	—
7. School Secretary	40	18,439	—	—	—	18,439	—	—	—
8. Program Manager	40	52,791	52,791	—	—	—	—	—	—
9. Social Worker	40	26,915	13,158	—	—	13,757	—	—	—
10. Clinical Supervisor	40	53,331	53,331	—	—	—	—	—	—
11. Social Worker	40	28,747	28,747	—	—	—	—	—	—
12. Social Worker	40	29,905	14,629	—	—	15,276	—	—	—
13. Social Worker	40	30,583	30,583	—	—	—	—	—	—
14. Exec. Director/Principal	40	62,133	—	—	—	62,133	—	—	—
15. Teacher	20	10,768	—	—	—	10,768	—	—	—
16. Teacher	40	27,685	—	—	—	27,685	—	—	—
17. Teacher Aide	40	15,576	—	—	—	15,576	—	—	—
18. Counseling Supervisor	20	16,616	16,616	—	—	—	—	—	—
19. Line Counselor	40	17,708	17,708	—	—	—	—	—	—
20. Line Counselor	40	16,082	16,082	—	—	—	—	—	—
21. Counseling Supervisor	20	20,497	20,497	—	—	—	—	—	—
22. Activities Counselor	40	22,113	22,113	—	—	—	—	—	—
23. Maintenance Supervisor	40	32,050	19,550	—	—	8,012	4,488	—	—
24. Maintenance	40	15,440	10,808	—	—	4,632	—	—	—
25. L.P.N.	40	41,784	41,784	—	—	—	—	—	—
26. Clinical Psychologist	40	87,016	—	—	2,323	—	37,734	6,312	40,647
27. Child Care Counselor	10	6,264	—	—	—	—	—	—	6,264
28. Overtime	0	139,989	57,089	9,915	351	31,165	27,435	6,971	7,063
Total Salaries		$929,732	$436,243	$75,768	$2,674	$238,145	$69,657	$53,271	$53,974

BUDGET CATEGORY	TOTAL	PROGRAM 1	PROGRAM 2	PROGRAM 3	PROGRAM 4	PROGRAM 5	PROGRAM 6	PROGRAM 7
FRINGES								
1. FICA	$71,125	$33,373	$5,796	$205	$18,218	$5,329	$4,075	$4,129
2. SUI	19,432	9,369	1,476	851	4,499	1,488	525	1,224
3. SDI	–	–	–	–	–	–	–	–
4. Workers' Compensation	43,512	20,460	2,982	69	13,262	2,695	2,322	1,722
5. Medical Insurance	87,113	23,229	1,416	495	34,769	7,266	13,883	6,055
6. Life Insurance	2,249	607	58	132	487	423	216	326
7. Pension Plan	–	–	–	–	–	–	–	–
Total Fringes	223,431	87,038	11,728	1,752	71,235	17,201	21,021	13,456
Total Salaries	929,732	436,243	75,768	2,674	238,145	69,657	53,271	53,974
Total Personnel	$1,153,163	$523,281	$87,496	$4,426	$309,380	$86,858	$74,292	$67,430

EXHIBIT E.1 Sample Detailed Organizationwide Expense Budget by Program *(continued)*

Budget Category	Total	Program 1	Program 2	Program 3	Program 4	Program 5	Program 6	Program 7
Consultants and Professional Services								
1. Management Services	$29,940	$ –	$11,123	$151	$12,159	$ –	$5,941	$566
2. Psychologist	4,448	2,188	–	–	2,260	–	–	–
3. Psychiatrist	32,479	23,385	–	–	9,094	–	–	–
4. Legal	2,101	–	2,101	–	–	–	–	–
5. Audit and Accounting	19,737	–	7,857	261	7,309	–	3,266	1,044
6. Data	4,806	–	2,146	–	1,462	–	1,198	–
7. Internist M.D.	5,361	4,279	–	–	–	1,082	–	–
8. Pharmacist	278	228	–	–	–	50	–	–
9. Property Acquisition	–	–	–	–	–	–	–	–
10. Dietary	2,251	1,050	–	–	336	605	–	260
11. Joint Commission	3,120	1,560	–	–	1,560	–	–	–
12. Security	2,501	2,501	–	–	–	–	–	–
Total	$107,022	$35,191	$23,227	$412	$34,180	$1,737	$10,405	$1,870
Materials and Supplies								
1. Household and Maintenance	$28,442	$15,425	$744	$912	$4,637	$4,808	$361	$1,555
2. Office	13,769	438	4,714	37	7,030	–	1,376	174
3. Kitchen and Dining Room	5,040	1,847	1,015	–	1,409	769	–	–
4. Laundry	2,017	1,510	–	–	–	411	–	96
5. Education	9,242	–	–	–	9,242	–	–	–
6. Social Services	1,398	317	–	–	13	1,068	–	–
7. Recreational	467	314	–	–	–	138	–	15
8. Medical	3,373	1,677	–	37	14	1,450	–	195
9. Food—Clients	43,836	22,080	–	1,893	11,503	6,525	–	1,835
10. Food—Staff	7,029	–	3,449	–	2,281	–	971	328
Total	$114,613	$43,608	$9,922	$2,879	$36,129	$15,169	$2,708	$4,198

EXHIBIT E.1 Sample Detailed Organizationwide Expense Budget by Program (*continued*)

Budget Category	Total	Program 1	Program 2	Program 3	Program 4	Program 5	Program 6	Program 7
Facility Costs								
1. Rental of Space	$65,291	$16,695	$3,291	$ –	$27,821	$14,715	$2,769	$ –
2. Depreciation and Interest	6,289	3,549	–	2,740	–	–	–	–
3. Heating Oil	8,038	4,271	89	–	2,984	195	139	360
4. Electric	20,126	8,148	383	1,099	4,917	4,304	371	904
5. Carpentry and Plumbing	2,619	1,739	–	–	49	647	–	184
6. Painting and Decorating	3,181	1,476	58	140	1,075	232	32	168
7. Grounds	145	–	8	13	119	–	5	–
8. Liability and Umbrella Insurance	2,099	731	79	168	551	333	60	177
9. Rubbish and Snow Removal	3,831	1,947	68	127	797	553	71	268
10. Electrical Repairs	3,046	1,609	43	–	1,102	280	12	–
11. Real Estate Tax	4,349	1,092	–	740	221	2,296	–	–
Total	$119,014	$41,257	$4,019	$5,027	$39,636	$23,555	$3,459	$2,061
Specific Assistance to Clients								
1. Allowance	$18,276	$15,706	$ –	$1,638	$ –	$111	$ –	$821
2. Clothing	–	–	–	–	–	–	–	–
3. Recreation	48,772	23,023	–	6,462	2,812	11,004	–	5,471
4. Personal Hygiene	22,825	15,985	–	840	–	5,456	–	544
5. Vocational Incentive	–	–	–	–	–	–	–	–
Total	$89,873	$54,714	$ –	$8,940	$2,812	$16,571	$ –	$6,836

Budget Category	Total	Program 1	Program 2	Program 3	Program 4	Program 5	Program 6	Program 7
Other								
1. Travel and Transportation	$20,678	$8,435	$783	$1,932	$3,044	$2,897	$2,621	$966
2. Telephone and Leased Telephone Equipment	13,296	4,648	2,281	428	2,832	861	2,046	200
3. Training Conferences and Meetings	2,135	–	1,129	14	430	–	547	15
4. Dues and Subscriptions	4,226	–	1,784	27	1,684	–	716	15
5. Management Travel	7,351	–	1,763	–	802	–	4,786	–
6. Prof. Liability and Bonding Insurance	–	–	–	–	–	–	–	–
7. Staff Recruitment	4,655	–	2,931	8	496	–	1,015	205
8. Staff Physical Exams	4,764	–	2,505	61	743	–	1,221	234
9. Staff Mileage—Auto Expense	3,704	–	203	10	73	–	3,418	–
10. Depreciation	1,265	–	326	–	675	–	264	–
11. Interest	–	–	–	–	–	–	–	–
12. Vehicle Insurance	7,339	1,622	1,635	293	1,411	335	1,734	309
13. Postage	2,962	–	1,516	–	472	–	974	–
14. Community Relations	84	–	–	–	–	–	84	–
15. General Management Expense	2,518	–	1,010	8	1,344	–	102	54
Total	$74,977	$14,705	$17,866	$2,781	$14,006	$4,093	$19,528	$1,998

EXHIBIT **Blank Detailed Organizationwide**
E.2   **Expense Budget by Program**

Budget Category	Total	Program 1	Program 2	Program 3	Program 4	Program 5	Program 6	Program 7
A. Personnel								
B. Consultants and Professional Services								
C. Materials and Supplies								
D. Facility Costs								
E. Specific Assistance to Clients								
F. Other Costs								
G. Total Operating Costs								
H. Equipment (detail not shown)								
I. Total Cost								

**Blank Detailed Organizationwide
Expense Budget by Program** *(continued)*

Budget Category	Hours per Week	Total	Program 1	Program 2	Program 3	Program 4	Program 5	Program 6	Program 7
Personnel									
1.									
2.									
3.									
4.									
5.									
6.									
7.									
8.									
9.									
10.									
11.									
12.									
13.									
14.									
15.									
16.									
17.									
18.									
19.									
20.									
21.									
22.									
23.									
24.									
25.									
26.									
27.									
28.									
Total Salaries									

Budget Category	Total	Program 1	Program 2	Program 3	Program 4	Program 5	Program 6	Program 7
Fringes								
1. FICA	——	——	——	——	——	——	——	——
2. SUI	——	——	——	——	——	——	——	——
3. SDI	——	——	——	——	——	——	——	——
4. Workers' Compensation	——	——	——	——	——	——	——	——
5. Medical Insurance	——	——	——	——	——	——	——	——
6. Life Insurance	——	——	——	——	——	——	——	——
7. Pension Plan	——	——	——	——	——	——	——	——
Total Fringes	——	——	——	——	——	——	——	——
Total Salaries	——	——	——	——	——	——	——	——
Total Personnel	==	==	==	==	==	==	==	==

Budget Category	Total	Program 1	Program 2	Program 3	Program 4	Program 5	Program 6	Program 7
Consulting and Professional Services								
1.								
2.								
3.								
4.								
5.								
6.								
7.								
8								
9.								
10.								
11.								
12.								
Total								
Materials and Supplies								
1.								
2.								
3.								
4.								
5.								
6.								
7.								
8								
9.								
10.								
Total								

BUDGET CATEGORY	TOTAL	PROGRAM 1	PROGRAM 2	PROGRAM 3	PROGRAM 4	PROGRAM 5	PROGRAM 6	PROGRAM 7
FACILITY COSTS								
1.								
2.								
3.								
4.								
5.								
6.								
7.								
8								
9.								
10.								
Total								
SPECIFIC ASSISTANCE TO CLIENTS								
1.								
2.								
3.								
4.								
5.								
Total								

BUDGET CATEGORY	TOTAL	PROGRAM 1	PROGRAM 2	PROGRAM 3	PROGRAM 4	PROGRAM 5	PROGRAM 6	PROGRAM 7
OTHER								
1.								
2.								
3.								
4.								
5.								
6.								
7.								
8.								
9.								
10.								
11.								
12.								
13.								
14.								
15.								
Total								

Miscellaneous Budgeting Checklists and Examples

Contents

EXHIBIT F.1   **Sample Introduction to the Budgeting Package**

The Board of Directors of our organization met last year in June to review and discuss the short- and long-term trends affecting the future of our organization. One of the Board's major conclusions was that, in order to preserve our financial viability, we must maintain programs most needed by our community in an efficient, low-cost manner.

The budgeting process is a vital means of attaining this goal. The budget becomes more than just an annual spending plan when it is developed through a process that involves careful consideration of:

1. Our mission
2. How that mission is translated into programs and services by the departments
3. The level of resources required to provide those programs and services efficiently and effectively

In such a case, the budget also functions as a long-range financial plan and operations guide. Thus, in its final form, the budget becomes an effective means of communicating our mission, goals, programs, and activities to our staff, community, and other interested parties.

This budget manual provides the necessary forms and instructions to complete departments' operating budget requests for 19XX.

THE OVERALL BUDGET PROCESS

Phase I: The Budget Policy and Strategy Phase

A. Our Mission Statement established by the Board of Directors and management sets the tone for budget development. It establishes the focus and direction for all programs and activities undertaken by our organization and departments.

B. The Board and management may elect to establish specific, short-term policies for the budget year, such as placing increased emphasis on particular programs or services, setting guidelines for operating budgets, and identifying general revenue trends or constraints affecting us.

C. The "Budget Kickoff" meeting held in November includes a presentation of major policy initiatives, guidelines, and directives. At this time, departments can obtain general policy information and seek clarification of how policies may affect their particular departments.

Phase II: Development of Budget Requests

A. Within the context of our Mission Statement and established policy for the budget year, departments are first asked to review and evaluate their own individual purposes and the programs and services required to pursue them. These may be reassessed and reprioritized by the department based on current or projected needs or other conditions.

B. Next, each department is required to prepare a thorough analysis and projection of all revenues expected for the budget year.

C. Then, after careful consideration of the department mission, priorities for service, and available resources, each department is required to set specific and measurable objectives for the coming year and establish performance measures for each objective.

D. The final step in developing the budget request is preparing the line-item expenditure budget. Each department is required to request the amounts it believes will be needed to support proposed activities for the budget year. In addition, departments are required to provide detailed information on the justification and projected costs for any new or expanded programs or services and for any new positions requested in the budget.

EXHIBIT F.1   **Sample Introduction to the Budgeting Package *(continued)***

Phase III: **Budget Review**

    A. All department budget requests are reviewed by the Finance Department. Departmental staff are responsible for identifying major issues and new or expanded programs or new programs in their budgets. In the event that further information or clarification is needed, appropriate staff members of the departments are contacted, and written clarification may be requested.

    B. All draft budgets are reviewed. A meeting will be held with each department to discuss the draft budget, answer questions, and provide any additional information or supporting documentation they believe necessary to explain and justify their budget fully. Follow-up meetings may be held if required.

Phase IV: **Budget Approval**

    A. At the conclusion of all budget meetings with department representatives, the final allocation decisions are made, and the recommended budget is presented to the Finance Committee.

    B. The Committee reviews recommended department budgets and forwards the final recommended budget to the Board of Directors for final approval.

Phase V: **Budget Dissemination**

    A. After Board approval, each department receives a copy of its approved budget.

    B. If departments have any questions concerning changes made to their requested budgets in the course of the review process, they should contact the Finance Department.

Phase VI: **Budget Monitoring**

    A. The approved expenditures, revenues, and objectives budgeted for each department form the basis for a system to monitor departmental performance and report variances of actual experience from budgeted amounts during the course of the year.

    B. Department staff should monitor actual revenues and expenditures versus budgeted revenues and expenditures on a monthly basis.

    C. Quarterly (or monthly if directed to do so) reports identifying budgeted versus actual variances are prepared by the Finance Department and distributed to departments for review and feedback.

    D. In the case of revenue projected to be under budgeted amounts or expenditures projected to exceed budgeted amounts, a departmental plan for corrective action is required, stating what actions the department will take to increase actual revenues or decrease the rate of expenditures. Corrective action plans are also required if monitoring indicates that stated objectives may not be attained during the year.

EXHIBIT F.2   Checklist for Effective Mission Statements

If you can answer each of the following statements affirmatively, the odds are that your nonprofit is on the right track when it comes to developing, using, and updating its mission statement:

☐ 1. Our nonprofit has a written mission statement.
- It is brief (no more than three clear sentences).
- It emphasizes what our organization wants to accomplish overall (its reason for existence).
- It avoids emphasizing how we intend to carry out our mission (specific activities, methods, goals, and programs).
- It avoids jargon and overly fancy language.
- It is clear, concise, and understandable to people *inside* our organization.
- It is clear, concise, and understandable to potential funding sources and donors *outside* the organization.
- It seems realistic, believable, and doable to people inside and outside the organization.

☐ 2. Board, management, and staff were involved in developing our mission statement.
- Board, management, and staff agree with it.
- They understand it and can summarize it accurately in conversation.

☐ 3. Our mission statement is referred to frequently within the organization.
- We use it to guide planning, goal setting, and program development.
- Board, management, and staff refer to it and regularly use it as a touchstone when they plan and make decisions.

☐ 4. Our mission statement is regularly reviewed in relation to our organization's programs and actual accomplishments.
- Board, management, and staff are involved in reviewing it.
- It is updated or modified as needed.
- Board, management, and staff are involved whenever it is updated or modified.

☐ 5. After reading our mission statement, everyone can tell what our nonprofit's unique mission is all about.

EXHIBIT F.3   **Sample Program Change Request Form**

REQUEST FOR NEW PROGRAM OR CHANGE TO EXISTING PROGRAM

This form requires detailed information on new programs or substantial changes to existing programs. A separate form must be completed for each new program or change to an existing program requested in the budget.

A. Program Title: Enter the name of the program and indicate whether it is a new program or a change to an existing program or service.

B. Program Summary: Provide a brief summary of the nature and purpose of the program or change and document the need for the program or change.

C. Anticipated Benefits and Outcomes: Identify the specific positive benefits or outcomes expected from the program. These could include:

- Cost reductions or revenue enhancements (or both)

- Improved client services

- Other outcomes that will contribute to the overall success of our organization

D. Three-Year Incremental Revenues and Incremental Expenses: Provide an estimate of the revenues and expenditures associated with the program or change over a three-year period:

- Revenues and expenditures must be stated incrementally (i.e., the amount in excess of the current year's budgeted revenues or expenditures).

- Revenues must be specifically identified (by source and amount) and verifiable.

- Expenditures must accurately reflect the total cost of the new program.

E. New Positions and Capital Equipment: Identify any new positions or capital acquisitions required in conjunction with the new program or change to an existing program.

ABC Corporation

_____ Budget

Request for New Program or Change to Existing Program

Department: _____   Date: _____

Prepared by: _____   Telephone: _____

Title: _____

Program Title: _____   Effective date: _____

☐ New Program   ☐ Change to Existing Program

Program Summary and Needs Analysis

_____

_____

_____

_____

_____

| EXHIBIT F.3 | Sample Program Change Request Form *(continued)* |

Anticipated Benefits and Outcomes

_____

_____

_____

_____

_____

_____

Fiscal Impact

INCREMENTAL REVENUES:	FY 1	FY 2	FY 3
1. _____	_____	_____	_____
2. _____	_____	_____	_____
3. _____	_____	_____	_____
4. _____	_____	_____	_____
Total Revenue:	_____	_____	_____

INCREMENTAL EXPENDITURES:	FY 1	FY 2	FY 3
1. Salaries and Wages	_____	_____	_____
2. Fringe Benefits	_____	_____	_____
3. Supplies	_____	_____	_____
4. Capital Equipment	_____	_____	_____
Total Expenditures:	_____	_____	_____

New Positions Required (Complete Exhibit F.4—New Position Request Form):

_____

EXHIBIT F.4   **New Position Request Form**

Department: _____

Prepared by: _____   Date: _____

Title: _____   Telephone: _____

☐ Union   ☐ Non-Union

Position Title: _____   Effective Date: _____

Total Hours: _____   Cost Center: _____

Describe the tasks and responsibilities of the requested position.

_____

_____

_____

_____

Demonstrate the need for the position, including relevance to the organization's mission and strategic plan. Use relevant workload statistics or other documented evidence of the need for the services to be provided.

_____

_____

_____

_____

Fiscal Impact

INCREMENTAL REVENUES:	FY 1	FY 2	FY 3
1. _____	_____	_____	_____
2. _____	_____	_____	_____
3. _____	_____	_____	_____
4. _____	_____	_____	_____
Total Revenue:	_____	_____	_____

INCREMENTAL EXPENDITURES:	FY 1	FY 2	FY 3
1. Salaries and Wages	_____	_____	_____
2. Fringe Benefits	_____	_____	_____
3. Supplies	_____	_____	_____
4. Capital Equipment	_____	_____	_____
5. Other	_____	_____	_____
Total Expenditures:	_____	_____	_____